D1549946

A-Z OF FESTIVALS

ROB da BANK'S
A-z of Festivals

MY LIFE OF MUSIC, MUD AND MAYHEM IN 26 LETTERS

ILLUSTRATIONS BY Josie da Bank

For the future festival folk Arlo and Merlin,
and any others on the way...

BOXTREE

First published 2009 by Boxtree, an imprint of Pan Macmillan Ltd
Pan Macmillan, 20 New Wharf Road, London N1 9RR
Basingstoke and Oxford, Associated companies throughout the world, www.panmacmillan.com

ISBN 978-0-7522-2700-9

Copyright (c) Rob da Bank Services Limited 2009

The right of Rob da Bank to be identified as the author of this work has been asserted by him in accordance with the Copyright, Designs and Patents Act 1988.

All rights reserved. No part of this publication may be reproduced, stored in or introduced into a retrieval system, or transmitted, in any form, or by any means (electronic, mechanical, photocopying, recording or otherwise) without the prior written permission of the publisher. Any person who does any unauthorized act in relation to this publication may be liable to criminal prosecution and civil claims for damages.

9 8 7 6 5 4 3 2 1

A CIP catalogue record for this book is available from the British Library.

Words by Rob da Bank
Illustrations by Josie da Bank
Design by Luke Lobley www.lukelobley.com
Additional words and research by Kieran Wyatt, Jonathan Lee, Simon Astall, Daniel Stevens, Ruby Warrington
Project co-ordinated by Ben Turner www.graphitemedia.net
Printed by Trento, Italy

This book is sold subject to the condition that it shall not, by way of trade or otherwise, be lent, re-sold, hired out, or otherwise circulated without the publisher's prior consent in any form of binding or cover other than that in which it is published and without a similar condition including this condition being imposed on the subsequent purchaser.

Visit www.panmacmillan.com to read more about all our books and to buy them. You will also find features, author interviews and news of any author events, and you can sign up for e-newsletters so that you're always first to hear about our new releases.

rite a book? Like the wife and I have got six months to spare. Nowt else to do chez the da Banks apart from run two festivals, programme two radio shows, A&R a record label, run a publishing company, bring up two kids and do the washing up! OK, so I always have actually harboured a desire to write a book but I was imagining hanging up my headphones at 45, moving to a small remote island off Jamaica with the family and penning a novel in the style of Ernest Hemingway (with a dash of Dick Francis thrown in for good measure). 'But it's a book about festivals,' said my manager Ben, knowing exactly the right buttons to press because festivals matter a lot to us, more than they should and more than is healthy. They're worth spending time talking about.

You know the feeling of seeing the first signs for the festival from the road or the twinkling glow of campfires. You've no doubt joined the slow moving but strangely companionable traffic jams, where a box of wine and some fancy dress suddenly appears on the back seat. The make-believe towns that we enter every time we go to a festival are the reason we love festivals so much; leave your worries at the gate, meet a load of randoms, get a bit mashed up and dance like there's no tomorrow. And then do it all again the next day.

I remember Josie and I going to our first Glastonbury and wishing that I could live there. Once I'd sobered up and realised I needed a shower, we headed home – but only until the next time! We hope you discover new festivals through this book and learn more about some that you love. And if you don't, then just stare at the beautiful drawings and get excited about festival season. See you in the queue for the overflowing toilet.

welcome

Merlin Arlo

the wonderful world of festivals......

CONTENTS

CONTENTS

A-Z OF FESTIVALS

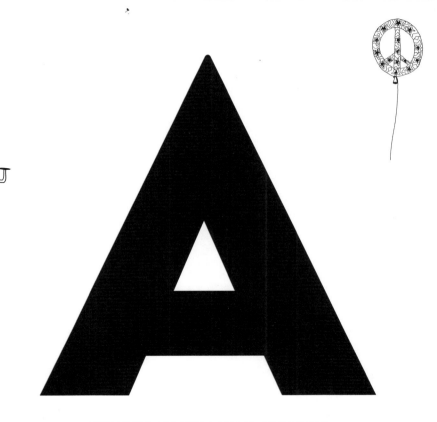

AIRWAVES **ALL TOMORROW'S PARTIES**
ASSOCIATION OF INDEPENDENT FESTIVALS ANGUS WATT
AREZZO WAVE **FIELD OF AVALON**

My quest to find a roast puffin was at an end. Here I was in the Icelandic capital, Reykjavik, for the tenth anniversary of the Airwaves festival and despite being vegetarian I was determined to find a restaurant that serves this traditional but rarely-eaten national dish. Puffin aside, I was having the time of my life. Three hours earlier I had been basking in one of the unofficial wonders of the world, the Blue Lagoon, a massive steaming sulphuric swimming pool heated by volcanic action. The nice folk at Airwaves had the inspired idea of getting some French rave DJs poolside and the whole lagoon had been partying in bikinis and shorts.

Reykjavik must be one of the smallest capital cities in the world (in fact, I hesitate to call it a city). But it's got some of the most happening niteries this side of New York. Over a fascinating hard-drinking weekend, I moshed to Bloc Party in an uber-modern art gallery, downed fiery Viking spirits to Late Of The Pier and discovered some incredible Icelandic bands. (Special mentions: Dr Spock, who like to wear washing-up gloves, and Mugison, who come on like guitar-wielding fishermen.) Add in fabulous art happenings and party people from Toronto and Tokyo and it's small surprise that Airwaves is now a permanent date in the da Bank diary.

AIRWAVES

Location: Reykjavik, Iceland **Founded:** 1999 **Current capacity:** 4,000 **Month:** October **Camping:** No **Nearest airport:** Keflavik
First headliners: GusGus, Thievery Corporation, Toy Machine **Recent headliners:** Vampire Weekend, CSS, Bloc Party **Promoter:** Mr Destiny
Website: www.icelandairwaves.com

'm sat on the floor of a poorly furnished chalet at 3am, arguing with a girl who says she doesn't like any vegetables. (Any! Ridiculous!) We're both incoherent on cheap cider and perishingly cold as we can't work the heating in this pesky space, but we've had such an inspirational weekend at All Tomorrow's Parties that frankly we couldn't care less. The British holiday camp Pontin's seems an unlikely home for one of the UK's most underground yet wildly popular weekenders. But when you can run around on a sandy beach by day then retire to a fake plastic olde English tavern for an ale before settling down to see a psychedelic array of live acts – roll up Yoko Ono, Suicide, Devendra Banhart, Portishead, Jerry Sadowitz and Aphex Twin – it all kind of makes sense. Until you try to find your way back to your chalet, that is.

With numerous annual happenings ranging from the UK's Nightmare Before Xmas extravaganza to sister events in New York and Australia, the key to ATP's success is its inspired choices of curators. Musicians Nick Cave and Sonic Youth, artists Jake and Dinos Chapman and even The Simpsons creator Matt Groening have all helmed proceedings at some point or other.

With no chance of mud, a fiercely loyal crowd and a manifesto pledging (and delivering) 'intimate, uncorporate and fan-friendly events', it's high time you joined the party too.

ALL TOMORROW'S PARTIES

Location: Pontin's, Camber Sands/Butlins, Minehead, UK **Founded:** 2000 **Current capacity:** 3,000 Camber/5,500 Minehead **Month:** Two weekends in May, one ('The Nightmare Before Christmas') in December **Camping:** Heated chalets **Nearest airports:** Heathrow/Gatwick, Bristol for Minehead **First curator:** Mogwai **Recent curators:** Portishead, My Bloody Valentine **Promoter:** ATP **Website:** www.atpfestival.com

Not to be confused with the Australian Institute of Fitness or the Amsterdam Institute of Finance, the Association of Independent Festivals was set up by yours truly and my manager Ben Turner in 2008. After three years of the notion buzzing around my brain that truly independent festivals in the UK needed a group to help and represent them in an increasingly cut-throat marketplace, we finally launched with a high-profile board of 13 members, including The Big Chill, Creamfields, WOMAD, Electric Picnic and Glade festivals.

With early aims to combat tent theft at UK festivals, get all our independent festies going green or greener and generally providing a forum to keep small festivals afloat and informed, AIF has been gradually building in terms of the number of festivals involved and being invited to all the right places/meetings/debates.

With a recession now kicking in across the world and obvious worries about festival numbers being hit, cost cutting and sharing of knowledge and talent is becoming even more vital for the small fish in the sea of festivals out there. We've taken cues from Yourope, the European Festival Association (www.yourope.org), which is now in its tenth year and with more than 50 members has been doing sterling work, especially with regard to festival safety and environmental issues.

AIF was launched in conjunction with the Association of Independent Music and if we can create half the change they have achieved for recorded music, this non-profit venture will have been worth the effort.

www.aiforg.com

'Angus has been "making dynamic and inspirational flags since 1993 to create a unique land-art form"; frankly, this is the kind of job I quite fancy doing'

Angus Watt is a familiar fixture at many festivals, from Glastonbury and WOMAD to my very own Bestival. An unassuming curly-haired chap, you'll often see him lugging scaffold poles in each arm (I once tried this myself and nearly ripped both my arms off attempting to pick them up). Ask Angus about his flags and you won't get monosyllabic mutterings but instead a treatise on the art of flag making and an in-depth insight into how to flock flags together to create not only beautiful spaces within a festival but also works of art in their own right. Speaking personally, Bestival certainly wouldn't look such a colourful and stimulating place without Angus's art.

On his website Angus says he has been 'making dynamic and inspirational flags since 1993 to create a unique land-art form'; frankly, this is the kind of job I quite fancy doing. Yet although it might sound easy to just knock up some flags and tour some of the world's best festivals – Rocket in the wilds of Spain or the festival of drumming in Colombo, Sri Lanka where local artists joined him in creating the flags – Angus actually spends months researching festival sites, sourcing different patterns, dying silk and making all the flags himself in the UK and Spain. And he's showing no signs of flagging. Sorry. www.anguswatt.net

AREZZO WAVE

Location: Livorno, Italy **Founded:** 1987 **Current capacity:** 30,000 **Month:** July **Camping:** No **Nearest airport:** Pisa **First headliner:** Sandro Oliva E Blue Pampurius **Recent headliners:** Chemical Brothers **Promoter:** Fondazione Arezzo Wave Italia **Website:** www.italiawave.com

Founded as a showcase for unsigned Italian talent, this Tuscan fixture has morphed into a full-blown multi-cultural feast, offering more than 180 events over four days spanning rock, classical and techno, theatre and watersports. A moniker change (it's now known as Italia Wave Love Festival) and a shunt east from the quaint confines of Arezzo to the buzzy port of Livorno reflect its coming of age: international acts have included Nitin Sawhney and the Kaiser Chiefs; there are also areas devoted to the spoken word and comics. Entry is free!

FIELD OF AVALON

Location: Worthy Farm, Somerset, UK **Founded:** 1985 **Current capacity:** 10.000 **Month:** June **Camping:** Yes **Nearest airports:** Bristol/Exeter **First headliner:** Kangaroo Moon **Recent headliners:** The Proclaimers, Katie Melua, **Promoter:** Field of Avalon **Website:** www.fieldofavalon.co.uk

If Glastonbury sums up everything that's right about festival culture, then its Field of Avalon space captures the freewheeling spirit down to a T. A sort of festival-within-a-festival, Avalon features folk and roots musicians, Morris dancers, site installations and craft sessions, all wrapped up in a near-horizontal, mystical atmosphere. Best of all, impromptu jams spring up all over the place, featuring musicians plucking, banging and blowing on a plethora of traditional instruments. Avalon tends to attract a particularly devoted breed of festival-goer, some not even venturing outside the confines of the space for the entire duration of the main Glastonbury event itself. It's all about the vibes, maaan, so don your velvet loon pants and magic mushroom felt hat and drift downstream!

BESTIVAL BURNING MAN THE BIG CHILL
FESTIVAL INTERNACIONAL DE BENICÀSSIM BONAROO BIG DAY OUT
BOOM BACK II LIFE BEAUTIFUL DAYS BRICK LANE

BESTIVAL

Location: Robin Hill Country Park, Isle Of Wight, UK **Founded:** 2004 **Current capacity:** 35,000 **Month:** September **Camping:** Yes **Nearest airports:** Bembridge/Southampton **First headliners:** Basement Jaxx, Fatboy Slim, Zero 7 **Recent headliners:** Amy Winehouse, Kraftwerk, My Bloody Valentine **Promoter:** Sunday Best/Get Involved **Website:** www.bestival.net

S ketched out on the back of a beer mat with a couple of bottles of wine inside the da Bank belly, Bestival was literally a slightly drunken pipedream. A dozen years of putting on Sunday Best parties – which started with two men and a dog in a bar in south London and had grown to co-hosting stages at Glastonbury – somehow gave us the confidence to put on our own festival. We wanted to create a beautiful, eccentric, non-corporate, colourful, chaotic, Alice in Wonderland meets the Wickerman meets Woodstock three-day extravaganza for both strange, dressed-up party people and real music fans who wanted more than a stage in a field with some lukewarm lager.

At the time, me and Josie da Bank and our partners John and Ziggy didn't really know what we were doing – and some say we still don't! We had in our mind's eye a psychedelic garden fête for a few hundred souls that would cost a couple of grand – and we found the perfect natural valley site at Robin Hill country park on the Isle of Wight.

I remember the night of the first show in 2004. With a better than expected 5,000 turning up to the gates, we suddenly realised as night fell that we had no overnight staff – so Josie and I spent all night going round politely asking people to turn off the 10k rig they'd set up in the woods, stop the burning toilet rolls being rolled into the

'With budgets running into millions, spiralling costs, recessions, more competition and fewer bands on the road, trying to keep the show on the straight and narrow is like balancing eggs on your head. But we can't and won't give it up'

lakes/ducks/highly flammable tents and generally requesting that attendees didn't kill anyone before dawn.

Morris dancers jigged about, cider was swilled, an inflatable church sat atop the hill hosting fake weddings, a huge wicker animal built over the festival weekend turned into a giant frog, Basement Jaxx ripped a hole in the sky with their greatest hits and our little pipedream became a living, breathing miniature community.

With one year under our belt we imagined it was time to put our feet up, dream about next year's headliners and put the deposit down on that yacht in Antigua – but six years on we're still getting to grips with it. With budgets running into millions , spiralling costs, recessions, more competition and fewer bands on the road, trying to keep the show on the straight and narrow is like balancing eggs on your head. But we can't and won't give it up.

Having the chance to book musical heroes such as Lee Scratch Perry, My Bloody Valentine, Kraftwerk and the Human League and bring in acts including Bat For Lashes, Dan le Sac vs Scroobius Pip and Lily Allen to bigger audiences is rewarding in itself. But seeing 30,000 people pogo to 'Born Slippy', witnessing Howard Marks DJ to a field full of trippy pirates, sliding down a hill in a rubber dinghy with a half-naked nun and watching the smiley faces keep beaming come rain or shine is what keeps Bestival ticking along. See you down the front.

Burning Man is less a festival, more a radical experiment in survivalism and free expression. Thousands of crazies camp out in high summer in 120-degree heat for seven days of music, art and life-changing experiences. Stories are legion of first-time attendees who subsequently jacked in their regular jobs for a life of nomadism and giving the finger to The Man.

The event takes place in the Nevada Desert, on an ancient lake-bed known as the Playa. It's a scene oft-compared to the Mad Max films, all mutant clothing, post-apocalyptic art and thousand-yard stares. People come to create – installations made of straw hats, music made from tent poles, audio broadcasts for the festival's Radio Free Burning Man station – and the event culminates on the Saturday night with the torching of a 40-foot-high wickerman, accompanied by a 50,000-strong chant of 'Burn him! Burn him!'.

You need to be prepared; Burning Man is an entirely self-sufficient exercise. Water, food and camping gear are rock-bottom essentials but many participants come fully loaded with RVs, bicycles, costumes, portable showers, cooking stoves and much more. If you rock up in a Hawaiian shirt and a pair of comedy flip-flops, you simply won't be let in. And there is absolutely nothing for sale on the Playa; trading and bartering are the order of the day.

From its origins in 1986 on a beach in San Francisco, Burning Man has come a long way. But it still marches to the beat of a different drummer and remains one of the most original festival experiences around.

BURNING MAN

Location: Black Rock Desert, Nevada, USA **Founded:** 1986 **Current capacity:** 50,000 **Month:** August **Camping:** Yes **Nearest airport:** Reno International **First headliner:** None **Recent headliners:** None **Promoter:** Black Rock City, LLC **Website:** www.burningman.com

another planet

Burning Man

YOU ARE HERE TO PARTICIPATE, BREATHE ART
DRINK WATER IN 107 DEGREES, TO CREATE
WEAR SUNBLOCK, BUILD A SHELTER, FIND LOVE
DRESS UP, TO CELEBRATE, BURN THE MAN
BE INDIVIDUAL

HOT

Black Rock DESERT

The Big Chill does what it says on the tin – a relaxing trip downstream in a hazy, slow-motion mix of electronica, throbbing dub and wacky jazz horns amid a kaleidoscopic cross section of babies, OAPs and 30-somethings. It's chilled without being polite, it's innovative without being pompous and it's exciting without being a rave. While many seasoned Big Chill campers prefer to hang out with their chums and a bottle of wine at the campsite during the day and the early evenings can resemble a pram parade as parents go for a pre-rave stroll with their kids, there are still those who scream about the site in gay abandon, dressing up to the nines in fancy dress and trying out the local brain-zapping cider.

One of the first festivals to have a strong green policy, the Chill has led the charge of the boutique festival ever since it started in the Welsh Black Mountains way back in 1995. It later moved to the Larmer Tree Gardens, where you'd walk around a ruined castle before encountering a peacock's fantail shimmying up the meticulously manicured path in front of you. Meanwhile, Mr Scruff busted out another sonic jazz gem.

Now in its fifteenth year, The Big Chill is firmly ensconced in its beautiful Eastnor Castle home. It is still a bastion of independent festivalling, complete with a vibrant online community, fantastic arts trail, sublime site and damn near-perfect weather every year. We raise a glass to its continued chilling.

THE BIG CHILL

Location: Eastnor Castle Deer Park, Herefordshire, UK **Founded:** 1994 **Current capacity:** 40,000 **Month:** August **Camping:** Yes **Nearest airports:** Birmingham/Bristol **First headliners:** Tom Middleton, Coldcut, Mixmaster Morris **Recent headliners:** Leonard Cohen, Basement Jaxx, Orbital **Promoter:** The Big Chill Group **Website:** www.bigchill.net

Not so much a festival, more a nine-day bender-cum-holiday, this event offers the opportunity to spend your nights dancing like a loon to top indie pop, rock and electronica outfits such as Babyshambles, Tricky and Mika and your days recovering on the beach. Promoters Maraworld have created the country's biggest festival: what started as a low-key bash attracting 8,000 ears-glued-to-the-underground hipsters now draws more than 100 artists and thousands of happy campers, who flood into a sleepy seaside town on the Costa del Azahar for a riotous and multifarious cultural fix. It has created such a noise that former Mean Fiddler festival promoter Vince Power took a large shareholding in the event. In true Iberian style, tunes run from 5pm to 8am (over four days) leaving punters to devote daylight hours to checking out short films, theatre, fashion shows and flamenco moves or, God forbid, sleeping (camping is free for all multi-day pass holders). Every square inch of the place is utilized: Benicàssim's beaches are littered with 'interventions' – Kenneth Russo's 2008 work was a piano floating on a red carpet off the shore – while artworks are displayed throughout the town.

Despite the cultural mix, music remains the prime attraction: comeback legends Brian Wilson and Morrissey have shuffled/strutted the festival stage while the likes of The Stone Roses, Jesus and Mary Chain, Massive Attack, Pet Shop Boys and Franz Ferdinand have all blown the crowds away. One for fireside tales with the grandkids.

FESTIVAL INTERNACIONAL DE BENICÀSSIM

Location: Benicàssim, Costa del Azahar, Spain **Founded:** 1995 **Current capacity:** 45,500 **Month:** July **Camping:** Yes **Nearest airport:** Valencia **First headliner:** The Charlatans **Recent headliners:** Oasis, Kings Of Leon **Promoter:** Maraworld/EOM **Website:** www.fiberfib.com

This festival may have been founded in 2002, but it's firmly rooted in the grow-your-own-hemp underpants vibe of the 1960s. Held on a 700-acre farm, the four-dayer is one of the few festivals to bag an Outstanding Greener Festival Award, impressing judges with everything from recycling and use of electric golf buggies to renewable energy production. It even has an on-site composter producing ten tonnes of the nutritious plant feed per event.

But where once it was lambasted for being too beardy-weirdy – Beck announced 'I smell hippies' during his 2006 set – festival organisers Superfly Productions and AC Entertainment have made a conscious effort to broaden the musical offering, pulling in big acts such as the Flaming Lips, Radiohead and Damian Marley. Punters can dip into everything from hip-hop, electronica, bluegrass and jazz to New Orleans funk, classic British rock and the all-female tribute band, Lez Zeppelin.

Beyond the main stages you'll find a 100-acre entertainment village featuring comedy and theatre, a beer festival and the bizarre attraction du jour, the silent disco. This smorgasbord of delights has helped secure the Billboard Touring Awards Top Festival medal four times. It's good to see the bongos and tie-dyed shirts haven't disappeared completely though: you can still check out yoga sessions at the solar-powered stage and prancing around in a field with a flute is actively encouraged.

BONNAROO MUSIC AND ARTS FESTIVAL

Location: Manchester, Tennessee, USA **Founded:** 2002 **Current capacity:** 80,000 **Month:** June **Camping:** Yes **Nearest airport:** Nashville
First headliner: Widespread Panic **Recent headliners:** Kanye West, Pearl Jam **Promoters:** AC Ents and Superfly **Website:** www.bonnaroo.com

BIG DAY OUT

Location: Auckland, Gold Coast (Southport), Sydney, Melbourne, Adelaide, Perth **Founded:** 1992 **Current capacity:** 282,692 **Month:** January/February **Camping:** No **Nearest airports:** Various **First headliner:** Nirvana **Recent headliners:** Arcade Fire, Dizzee Rascal, Unkle **Promoters:** Vivian Lees and Ken West **Website:** www.bigdayout.com

This juggernaut of a rawk festival (with a smidgen of indie and electronica) sees countless pairs of leather trousers swagger through six Antipodean cities. Entertainment runs from lighters-aloft living legends such as Neil Young to mosh-friendly gigs by Metallica and The Killers. Don't miss theatrics from the likes of Lightning For Hire (crackling four-million volt Tesla coils anyone?) or a wander through Lilyworld's psychedelic 'festival within a festival' with its nascent stars such as funkabilly's Barrence Whitfield and 80s pop throwbacks The Reels.

BOOM FESTIVAL

Location: Lake Idanha-a-Nova, Portugal **Founded:** 1997 **Current capacity:** 25,000 **Month:** August (held every other year) **Camping:** Yes **Nearest airport:** Lisbon **First headliner:** Quirk **Recent headliner:** Boxcutter **Promoter:** Good Mood **Website:** www.boomfestival.org

Welcome to Portugal's answer to a massive Goan love-in. Starting life as a psy-trance event, the week-long lakeside tribal-fest has embraced multi-media installations, landscape art, healing, ufology and Siberian Xamanism. (No, we're not sure either.) Organisers are firmly anti-populist, eschewing superstar DJs for a bill of neo-Goan and acoustic trance, world and ancestral tunes and other assorted cosmic beats. There's a good green tinge too: the event bagged a Greener Festival Award in 2008 and regularly showcases wonders such as the Scheffler mirror solar-powered kitchen.

'A lot of people go out there in little groups and come away as lifelong friends' – Norman Jay

Eight days on a Caribbean island with music supplied by some of the very best DJs in the UK. A tropical marine climate guaranteed to deliver blazing sunshine. Five-star hotels, all-night parties and downright good vibes. That's the Back II Life festival in Antigua in a nutshell. The question is: what's stopping you? Back II Life is the brainchild of four key players in the UK soundsystem scene: Soul II Soul's Jazzie B, dancehall don David Rodigan, Notting Hill carnival kingpin Norman Jay and Radio 1's Trevor Nelson. No matter if they're dropping reggae, dancehall, hip-hop, rare groove or house sounds, each DJ is guaranteed a rapturous reception wherever and whenever they play. Interspersed between the four main festival days are a host of intimate pool parties, villa parties, boat parties, beach parties and, er, plain old parties, all taking place against a backdrop seemingly stolen wholesale from *Fantasy Island*. Add in some tasty rum and massive tunes and it's no surprise that Norman Jay once said this: 'A lot of people go out there in little groups and come away as lifelong friends.'

BACK II LIFE

Location: Antigua, West Indies **Founded:** 2004 **Month:** April **Camping:** No **Nearest airport:** Antigua **First headliner:** Jazzie B
Recent headliners: Jazzie B, Norman Jay, David Rodigan **Promoters:** Soul II Soul **Website:** www.soul2soul.co.uk

BEAUTIFUL DAYS

Location: Escot Park, Ottery St Mary, Devon, UK **Founded:** 2003 **Current capacity:** 10,000 **Month:** August **Camping:** Yes **Nearest airport:** Exeter **First headliner:** The Levellers **Recent headliners:** The Levellers **Promoter:** The Levellers **Website:** www.beautifuldays.org

The family-friendly Beautiful Days festival was set up by anarcho-folk-rockers The Levellers as an alternative to what they saw as the over-commercialisation of the UK festival scene. Numbers are capped at just 10,000, making for an intimate and friendly atmosphere. The Majical Youth Theatre hosts a huge children's area right in the centre of the site, laying on activities such as face painting, dressing up, circus acts and theatre. The Levellers hand-pick the eclectic line-ups, which include comedians, walkabout performers and dub DJs.

BRICK LANE MUSIC FESTIVAL

Location: Brick Lane, London, UK **Founded:** 2008 **Current capacity:** 10,000 **Month:** September **Camping:** No **Nearest airports:** Gatwick/ Heathrow **First headliner:** Norman Jay **Promoter:** Vibe Bar **Website:** www.vibe-bar.co.uk

Four of east London's coolest watering holes – 93 Feet East, Vibe Bar, Café 1001 and the Big Chill Bar – come together for an all-day session of music, DJs, art, film, cabaret and performance. It all takes place on the eponymous Brick Lane, the epicentre of the UK's curry industry, and also marks the first day of the Banglatown International Curry Week, which see chefs flying in from the subcontinent to unleash the latest spicy recipes.

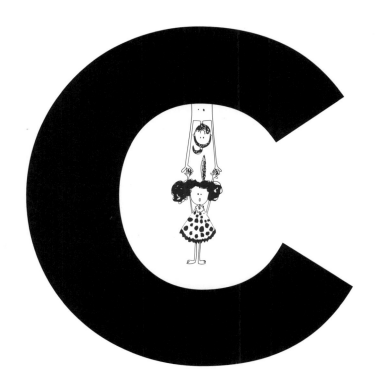

COACHELLA VALLEY MUSIC AND ARTS FESTIVAL
CAMBRIDGE FOLK FESTIVAL CAMP BESTIVAL CREAMFIELDS CONCRETE AND GLASS
FESTIVAL CENTRAL PARK SUMMERSTAGE CORNBURY MUSIC FESTIVAL

COACHELLA VALLEY MUSIC AND ARTS FESTIVAL

Location: Empire Polo Field, Indio, California, USA **Founded:** 1999 **Current capacity:** 50,000 **Month:** April **Camping:** Yes **Nearest Airport:** LAX **First headliners:** Beck, The Chemical Brothers, Rage Against The Machine **Recent headliners:** Paul McCartney, The Killers, The Cure **Promoter:** Goldenvoice/AEG Live **Website:** www.coachella.com

There I was, driving across the Nevada Desert in a gargantuan RV (that's an outsized camper van to me or you or anyone living outside of the USA), cruising along roads that demanded no turn of the wheel for tens of miles, stopping off at sand-whipped chrome diners for hubcap-sized burgers. I really couldn't have been happier. I was on my way, with the wife and our best mate T, to Coachella in 2004 and this was the way to arrive. If we'd dropped this elephantine vehicle onto the streets of London we'd have gotten stuck within minutes; but here, under the shimmering, metallic desert sky, we just set the autopilot to, er, auto and let the wheels take the strain. I'd make frequent arduous journeys from the passenger seat to the fridge for a cold beer in one of the plush swivelling armchairs as the cacti whizzed past outside.

As we passed the gigantic wind farms perched on arid cliffs outside Palm Springs, we started rehearsing our lines to blag our way into the backstage campsite at Coachella, the hip US music festival launched by Paul Tollett and his Goldenvoice company in 1999. My usual trick of just driving straight into the site without any kind of vehicle pass and pretending I was a rock star had worked three or four times at Glasters. (The one time it didn't was when I pretended to be one of The Stone Roses without realising they'd split up.) Surely they would go for

'Coachella has possibly the highest quota of real-life rock stars – complete with accompanying behemoth vehicles – and the rigid security looked at me like the scruffy English oik I was when we arrived in our dusty bedroom on wheels'

my quaint English accent and believe my sorry story. Sadly, Coachella has possibly the highest quota of real-life rock stars – complete with accompanying behemoth vehicles – and the rigid security looked at me like the scruffy English oik I was when we arrived in our dusty bedroom on wheels. Hours later, after we'd pitched ourselves up in a regular campsite, we sat shamefaced at not being able to beat the system but happy to be sat under the vast cascading celestial skies of Nevada.

With morning came our first venture onto the festival site and a scene as far removed from the English festival setting of burger vans axle-deep in mud, lines of overflowing portaloos and a stall selling herbal highs. Instead, leggy models tottered around the backstage area in high heels, Cameron Diaz and Drew Barrymore reclined on chaise longues supping cocktails out of real glass glasses and steroid-packed males strutted around with their pecs out like peacocks in the blazing sun. Meanwhile, us pasty Brits hid under a canopy, drinking far too quickly for midday, scanning the beautiful people for another Hollywood face. As it got cooler and the temperature dropped to a more sedate 100 degrees, we headed over to a Big Top to see Beck. We got within about half a mile of the outside of the tent and hit the back of the queue to see the troubadour.

'Leggy models tottered around the backstage area in high heels, Cameron Diaz and Drew Barrymore reclined on chaise longues supping cocktails and steroid-packed males strutted around with their pecs out like peacocks in the blazing sun'

Deciding to grab a drink on the way back across the pancake-flat parched grass of the polo field that hosts Coachella, we encountered some of the downsides of this party paradise. Local laws mean the public bars are caged off and once you've bought an alcoholic drink you can't leave the cage; this resulted in the oh-so-predictable scenario of us downing drinks at breakneck speed before moving across the field to the next enclosure. However, spotlight performances at the festival included a dark and brooding performance from The Cure and a tear-jerkingly sublime turn from Radiohead. Kraftwerk also thrilled with an indoor performance in a cavernous tent, fooling about with our minds with robots and giant visuals.

Recent appearances by Madonna and Prince confirm Coachella's undisputed ability to attract huge names and deliver stunning line-ups. Yes, there's something slightly too clinical for the crusty in da Bank in this flat land of caged bars, perfect smiles and giant camper vans stretching out in regimental lines. But I'll certainly be back as soon as I can, albeit without the RV.

ambridge Folk Festival was first staged in 1964, when the city council asked local man-about-town Ken Woollard to organise a groovy happening. Around 1,400 people attended, catching a glimpse of a very young Paul Simon who was added to the bill at the last minute. Woollard ran and grew the festival for the next 30 years, until his death in 1993 when Cambridge City Council Arts & Entertainments took over. These days, the four-day festival performs a delicate balancing act, mixing up established acts such as Joan Baez, Billy Bragg, Judy Collins and Joan Armatrading with more cutting-edge folkies like Tunng, Peatbog Faeries and The Imagined Village.

If you're expecting grimy toilets, stalls selling BSE burgers, gangs of knife-wielding muggers and other elements beloved of the typical British festival experience, then you're in for a pleasant surprise. Toilets tend to be queue-free for most of the weekend, there is plenty of space in which to roam around, staff are knowledgeable and friendly and the general air is of a place that time forgot. This, after all, is a festival where The Archers – a quaint soap about farmers broadcast on British radio – is piped in as a morning warm-up. Be prepared: tickets usually go on sale in May and the festival has sold out in advance for more than a decade.

CAMBRIDGE FOLK FESTIVAL

Location: Cherry Hinton Hall, Cambridge, UK **Founded:** 1964 **Current capacity:** 10,000 **Month:** August **Camping:** Yes **Nearest airport:** Stansted **First headliner:** Paul Simon **Recent headliners:** Joe Strummer, The Levellers, Joan Baez **Promoter:** Cambridge City Council Arts & Entertainments **Website:** www.cambridgefolkfestival.co.uk

CAMP BESTIVAL

Location: Lulworth Castle, Dorset, UK **Founded:** 2008 **Current capacity:** 15,000 **Month:** July **Camping:** Yes **Nearest airports:** Bournemouth

First headliner: Chuck Berry, Flaming Lips, Kate Nash **Recent headliners:** PJ Harvey, Bon Iver **Promoter:** Sunday Best/Get Involved

Website: www.campbestival.net

Some gossip-ridden website proclaimed 'Bestival to leave Isle of Wight', woefully misreading our new venture as an act of treason to our faithful chums on the island. In reality, we were simply starting a new, second show in Dorset but the festival grapevine is always humming with some exciting slander or other. It was early 2007 and myself and Mrs da Bank were enjoying a glass of red wine or four and discussing how we reckoned festivals are for all ages to enjoy. Slowly, without realising, the seeds were being sown for a new show from the Bestival camp: Camp Bestival! While the original Bestival has continued to attract all-comers – from breastfed babes in arms and hordes of rampant raving teens to thirsty 30-somethings and my 90-year-old grandfather – it had turned into too big and too loud a show for many families.

In fact, 2007 had been a very busy year for festivals and there'd been a lot of talk of saturation in the market, so we were either going to be very brave or very foolish to set up a new festival in 2008. But they say fortune favours the brave and after the third bottle of wine we were convinced that there was a small gap in the market for a festival with both a really great line-up and a site designed to revolve around families. The next bleary-eyed morning, Camp Bestival still seemed a good idea.

Boasting as diverse a line-up as the mothership Bestival (everyone from the 82-year-old Chuck Berry to the Wurzels and Hercules and Love Affair dropped by), Camp Bestival's raison d'etre revolves around the family. There's a humongous Kids Garden incorporating an insect circus, cardboard-castle workshops, dressing-up shops and children's theatre groups. The tented real ale pub, The Seaview Inn, was for the dads to sup their pints in while watching the kids muck about in the giant outdoor kindergarten. Miraculously, even with 3,000 under-12s present, the rest of the site doesn't feel over-run by little people and those who have come without children still fill their days and nights with Come Dancing lessons, karaoke, impromptu aerobics and a Mad Hatter's Tea Party organised by our very own Bestival Bluecoats. It all culminates in a good old-fashioned late-night rave-up to DJs such as Yoda and Gilles Peterson.

Personal highlights included Wayne Coyne (from Saturday headliners The Flaming Lips) clambering into his giant see-through Zorb sphere and tumbling down the steps of Lulworth Castle before bouncing across the crowd and jumping out onto the stage singing the first song. And then there were the weird and wonderful arty happenings in the beautifully-lit woods involving local theatre groups and the English National Ballet.

For the first year, we didn't get everything right and I still spent most of the weekend with a radio glued to my ear trying to sort out the toilet queues and pacify frustrated parents who were camped too far from said conveniences. But as I crashed out in our camper van four hours before our own kids started whacking me awake, the twilight festival hubbub of people shouting, the gentle thud of distant bassbins and the crackle of the campfires reminded me why we started another one. Roll on 2009 and beyond.

CREAMFIELDS

Location: Daresbury, Halton, Cheshire **Founded:** 1998 **Current capacity:** 40,000 per day **Month:** August **Camping:** Yes **Nearest airports:** Liverpool John Lennon/Manchester **First headliners:** Run DMC, Ian Brown, Daft Punk (DJ set) **Recent headliners:** Kasabian, The Prodigy, Massive Attack, Fatboy Slim **Promoter:** Cream Ltd **Website:** www.creamfields.com

love Creamfields. Coming from about as far south as you can get in the UK – Portsmouth, by its own admission starved of inspiring nightlife – my early visits to Liverpool's Cream club opened my eyes to the more hedonistic, glamorous and downright more in-ya-face glory of Northern clubbing in the 90s. Seeing the reverence with which DJs such as Paul Oakenfold were treated at Cream – not to mention the queues that would start hours before the club opened – showed me that Cream clubbers were serious about their music and dancing. Many a lost weekend started in the club's warehouse space, Nation, and finished days later in some hotel room in the city.

And long before there was a dance festival in every other field in the UK, there was Creamfields. Started in 1998 at the Matterley Bowl site in Winchester with former partner Darren Hughes, Creamfields was the natural outdoor brother of the Cream superclubbing phenomenon. Having celebrated a decade of dance in 2008, founder James Barton wanted to deliver a new kind of clubbing experience. It created a style of festival new to the UK circuit, one which attracted pink fluffy bras and boots to muddy fields.

'We wanted to turn what we'd achieved with the club into a festival,' says James. 'We had Ibiza but we didn't have an outdoor music event for out-and-out clubbers in the UK. We wanted to give all these kids who

'We wanted to turn what we'd achieved with the club into a festival. We had Ibiza but we didn't have an outdoor music event for out-and-out clubbers in the UK' – James Barton

loved dance music an opportunity to support something in the UK that stood for what they loved. And that continues to this day at our new home in Cheshire.'

The second year saw Creamfields return to its native Liverpool and 35,000 turned up to see the Pet Shop Boys headline a blistering weekend of fun in the sun. Barton says another highlight was the Scissor Sisters headlining in 2005. 'We booked them when they were unknown but by the week of the show the album was Number One. It was a case of lucky, perfect timing.' Having relocated to a new site in 2007 and shifted to a two-day camping format, Creamfields continues to broaden its appeal with more eclectic bookings.

I've had some mega times at Creamfields, hanging out with some of the most hardened music fans about and dancing till dawn. I also got to DJ there when I warmed up for DJ Shadow in 2006 – an incredible experience. And going to Creamfields in Buenos Aires during the Argentine financial collapse was inspiring, especially seeing thousands of young Argentines dancing under the scorching sun without a care in the world.

With Creamfields' continued advances into wider territories – there are now Creamfields in Spain, Poland, the Czech Republic, Mexico, Malta, Argentina, Chile, Romania, Brazil and Peru – this is one festival brand that is destined to be around for many years to come.

CONCRETE AND GLASS

Location: East London, UK **Founded:** 2008 **Current capacity:** Various **Month:** October **Camping:** No **Nearest airports:** Heathrow/Gatwick **First headliners:** Error, Telepathe, Heart Of Glass **Promoters:** Tom Baker and Flora Fairbairn **Website:** www.concreteandglass.co.uk

Concrete and Glass may be a relatively recent addition to London's urban festival culturescape and look scarily cool but it's still managed to launch on a hugely impressive scale: 100 bands and more than 20 exhibitions across 35 venues. A kind of London-based Sonar, the line-ups place a heavy emphasis on experimental and cutting edge talent rather than established names. There are also opportunities for budding culture-makers to make their mark, with an open art competition held in Shoreditch Town Hall. An arty farty party that we applaud.

CENTRAL PARK SUMMERSTAGE

Location: Rumsey Playfield, Central Park, New York, USA **Founded:** 1986 **Current capacity:** 10,000 **Month:** June/August **Camping:** No **Nearest airports:** John F Kennedy (JFK)/LaGuardia/Newark Liberty International **First headliners:** Sun Ra Arkestra, Olu Dara **Recent headliners:** Wyclef Jean, Sonic Youth, Cinematic Orchestra **Promoter:** City Parks Foundation **Website:** www.summerstage.org

Tailor-made for the cheeseparing urbanite, this festival offers a lively programme of tunes, spoken word and dance in the leafy surrounds of New York's Central Park. Most events are gratis – one of 2008's best freebies was a soul and funk fest featuring Sharon Jones and the Dap Kings – while other fixtures politely suggest a donation of a pocket-friendly $5. The aim is to connect the city's diverse communities and promote bright new talent, so stand by for performances of every hue from Israeli contemporary dance to opera, Latin, trip-hop, lounge, electro-funk and gospel. There's been a good showing of home-grown artists too, such as the Roy Hargrove Big Band.

f you're more barn dance than pills and pogoing, this rural festival has your name all over it. There's been a traditional fair on this idyllic Oxfordshire estate since 1796, but it's taken the keen ear of festival director Hugh Phillimore to update the formula to create a stomping weekender for our times. Morris dancers, farmers, fairground rides, craft stalls and real ale remain in the mix, while hot-air balloon trips, gourmet catering, kids' workshops, luxury showers and er, plugged-in instruments bring the whole shebang into the twenty-first century. Line-ups are entirely in keeping with the chilled out vibe: crowd pleasers such as Crowded House and 10cc mix with cult outfits like Half Man Half Biscuit and The Love Trousers. The nosh can't be faulted either, blending quality British produce from the likes of the Real Meat Sausage Company with Mexican, French and even Goan specialities.

The biggest boons, however are the canvas options. This is a proper camping festival so get in quick to book your very own king-size bamboo bed at the on-site Yurtel or, failing that, bag a tipi or 'podpad' – a fancy pre-erected tent that saves you grappling with billowing fly sheets in a force-ten gale.

The festival has earned its eco spurs too: carbon neutral motor insurance company Ibuyeco sponsored the 2008 event, offsetting CO_2 emissions produced by festival-goers arriving by car.

CORNBURY MUSIC FESTIVAL

Location: Cornbury Park, Charlbury, Oxfordshire, UK **Founded:** 2004 **Current capacity:** 20,000 **Month:** July **Camping:** Yes

Nearest airport: Heathrow **First headliner:** Paul Simon **Recent headliners:** Will Young, Blondie, Jools Holland **Promoter:** Sound Advice

Website: www.cornburyfestival.com

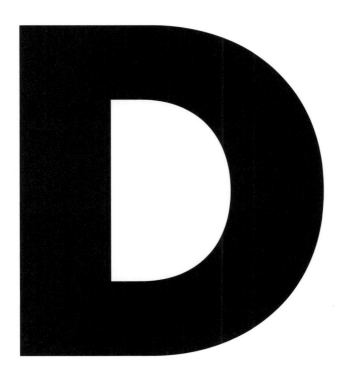

D

DRESSING UP DANCE VALLEY DOUR FESTIVAL DOWNLOAD FESTIVAL

Dressing up? At a festival? Not in my day, mate. That's what I'd have said six years; ago, a ravaged veteran of numerous Glastonburys, Readings and crusty raves in Essex woods. A pair of combat trousers and a day-glo builder's jerkin back in '89 perhaps, but I certainly wouldn't have spent months planning my fancy dress for a festival. Fast forward to today and it's all the rage. I suppose Bestival's partly to blame. With so many great festivals in the UK, we wanted to do something to help us stand out. Like so many of our crazy ideas, this one came about after a session of black Sambuccas had mashed our heads and we made the decision to throw the largest fancy dress party in the world at Bestival 2006.

With a bit of research into the Guinness Book Of Records, we found out that – miraculously – no such record existed. How civilisation has survived thousands of years without setting that record beats me, but we set out to beat the non-existent record anyway. Ten thousand people joined in that first parade, a veritable army of sea creatures, spacemen, baked-bean cans, naked Silver Surfers, a team of arctic explorers slow-motion walking across the site and (my favourite) a beautiful Indian girl 'standing' in a giant silver Indian takeaway container complete with the price scrawled on the top.

Of course, Bestival didn't invent dressing up at festivals. But the success of the fancy dress idea is a reflection of people's desire to step out of their usual clothes and lives – if only for a weekend.

Dubbed 'the Woodstock of dance', Dance Valley is where you go if you want to trance it up. The biggest names in the genre play at this, one of Europe's biggest outdoor techno events. British superjock Carl Cox has been a mainstay, headlining at both the inaugural event in 1995 and latterly in 2008. The festival is famous for its no-expense-spared approach to booking, often flying in DJs by private jet from Ibiza to ensure they can spin at the event. And although trance remains at the festival's heart, more than a dozen smaller tents and stages cater for electro, experimental, minimal house and harder styles in the idyllic nature reserve that is the Spaarnwoude Recreation Ground. The likes of British techno-punksters The Prodigy, Detroit techno icon Derrick May and New York house legend Danny Tenaglia illustrate the international flavour of the line-ups.

The main stage is housed in a natural valley – hence the name – and the event itself is known for its flawless organisation and attention to detail. If you perch yourself high up on the hill late at night, the view of the main stage below you is simply breathtaking – thousands of arms in the air, reaching out into a fog of lasers and dry ice to catch the invisible bagels shooting out of the speakers.

DANCE VALLEY

Location: Spaarnwoude, Netherlands **Founded:** 1995 **Current capacity:** 50,000 **Month:** July **Camping:** No **Nearest airport:** Amsterdam
First headliner: Carl Cox **Recent headliners:** Carl Cox, Richie Hawtin, Paul van Dyk, Tiësto **Promoter:** UDC **Website:** www.dancevalley.com

**W**ith a staggering 144,000 (and counting) capacity, the Dour festival is not only one of Europe's biggest but also almost single-handedly responsible for putting this oh-so-sleepy part of one of Europe's smaller countries on the cultural map. Certainly the pick'n'mix approach to music programming has boosted the festival's appeal, with something-for-everyone line-ups dominating year after year. There are plenty for dance heads, including the likes of Wu-Tang Clan, Richie Hawtin, Roni Size and DJ Shadow, but also much for those of a six-string persuasion, like The Fall, Black Rebel Motorcycle Club, Anthrax and Hot Chip.

Promoter Carlo Di Antonio is also a local politician, so it's small surprise that the festival donates large chunks of its profits to worthy causes, including Oxfam, Positive Economy and various cultural programmes. And there's a whiff of socialism about the ticket prices too – in 2008 a bargain £65/€85 for four days, including camping – meaning the event is insanely popular. In fact, in 2007 organisers turned away 15,000 ticketless would-be punters each day of the festival.

Dour certainly lives up to its billing as an alternative music festival and takes pride in giving a break to new and up-and-coming musicians and DJs. Don't be worried by the language barrier either; the catch-all greeting of 'Bon festival!' will ensure you make plenty of friends.

DOUR FESTIVAL

Location: Dour, Belgium **Founded:** 1989 **Current capacity:** 144,000 **Month:** July **Camping:** Yes **Nearest airport:** Paris Charles de Gaulle
First headliner: Bernard Lavilliers **Recent headliners:** Hot Chip, Wu-Tang Clan **Promoter:** Carlo Di Antonio **Website:** www.dourfestival.be

For those about to rock, we salute you. The Download festival is your chance to dig out the earplugs, crank up the amps to 11 and rock on at the loudest party on the planet (probably). We're talking heavy riffage and even heavier metal, with line-ups that regularly feature the biggest and ugliest bands around (think Metallica, Megadeth, Black Sabbath). You won't find any sad-case indie types staring embarrassingly at their shoes – 2005's 'indie day' is unlikely to be repeated – although more muscular janglers such as Feeder and Dinosaur Jr have more than held their own.

Download has been the scene of some controversy in the past – whiny Guns N'Roses frontman Axl Rose had bottles of piss thrown at him while UK grime star Lethal Bizzle was pelted with tubs of Müller Rice – but in general the vibe is good-natured, if heavy on the testosterone. The festival has also won stacks of awards, including a Billboard magazine gong for Top Festival of 2007.

Stand-out moments include Kiss singer Paul Stanley flying Superman-style across the crowd on a pulley system and Judas Priest's chief rabble rouser Rob Halford claiming to be Nostradamus while wearing a silver cloak and brandishing a pitchfork. Po-faced it ain't. The Download brand has also branched out into the US, staging concerts in San Francisco, Boston, Los Angeles and Philadelphia during 2008, with the emphasis on slightly less heavy acts such as Beck and Modest Mouse.

DOWNLOAD FESTIVAL

Location: Donington Park, Derbyshire, UK **Founded:** 2003 **Current capacity:** 45,000 **Month:** June **Camping:** Yes **Nearest airport:** Leicester **First headliner:** Iron Maiden **Recent headliners:** Lostprophets, The Offspring **Promoter:** Live Nation **Website:** www.downloadfestival.co.uk

EXIT ELECTRIC PICNIC eFESTIVALS

Exit is held in the Petrovaradin Fortress in Novi Sad in Serbia, a beautiful eighteenth-century building situated close to the Danube. For many it's an annual pilgrimage, a four-day shindig that sees attendees returning to their home countries in a right old state, all glassy-eyed, several kilos lighter and speaking in tongues. It's that kind of experience. Started by three university students in 2000, Exit has strong social and political undercurrents and admirably sticks to its philosophy of bringing the best music and culture to the Serbian youth, even as half of Manchester, Paris and Rome climb the walls for a look in. The first Exit in 2000 rumbled on for a mind-blowing 100 days at various locations around the city and was very much an anti-Milosevic protest, culminating days before the dictator was overthrown. Later festivals have been just as abnormal, with embezzlement charges (which were later dropped) against the promoters in one year and the Serbian minister of finance dropping by to play a set of weird cover versions the next.

Musically, expect a massively mixed bag, from Serbian faves Darko Rundek and KUD Idijoti to big hitters the Sex Pistols, MIA, Iggy Pop and The Wailers. Oh yes, and lots and lots of techno, from ear bleeding to ambient.

EXIT

Location: Petrovaradin Fortress, Novi Sad, Serbia **Founded:** 2000 **Current capacity:** 50,000 **Month:** July **Camping:** Yes **Nearest airport:** Belgrade **First headliners:** Finley Quaye, Kosheen, Roni Size **Recent headliners:** Sex Pistols, Primal Scream, Juliette Lewis **Promoter:** Exit **Website:** www.exitfest.org

A PLACE OF WILD FUN

SERBIA

novi sad
since
2001

EXIT

FESTIVAL

190,000

PEOPLE

E lectric Picnic (or our Irish cousins, as we call them at Bestival HQ) tends to fall the weekend before our show. This is great in that bands coming from the States or abroad can do two impactful gigs in September back to back but it's also terrible because many of the same crew, entertainers and food outlets do both events, meaning we witness a slow stream of very hungover, tired people turning up late to set up at Bestival! But no matter, Electric Picnic also shares many of the same values as Bestival: acts that punch above their weight for the size of the show (recent Picnics have welcomed Kraftwerk, Sonic Youth, New Order, The Flaming Lips and Sex Pistols), amazing value for money and a really eccentric crazy vibe. In fact there are few festies that get as simultaneously raucously drunk on the Friday night and then super chilled by the Sunday as EP.

Set in the wooded wonderland of Stradbally Hall in County Laois not far from Dublin, this boutique festival has had praise heaped on it with *Billboard* describing it as a 'textbook example of everything a festival should be'. We agree. From the music, comedy and madness on offer to the 24-hour cinema tent, the Body'n'Soul arena's ambient lounge replete with beanbags and tarot card readings and the Silent Disco pumping away into the Irish night, this really is the perfect Picnic.

ELECTRIC PICNIC

Location: Stradbally Hall, Stradbally, Co Laois, Ireland **Founded:** 2004 **Current capacity:** 32,500 **Month:** August/September **Camping:** Yes **Nearest airports:** Dublin **First headliners:** Groove Armada, Super Furry Animals, Grandmaster Flash **Recent headliners:** Kraftwerk, Nick Cave, My Bloody Valentine, Björk **Promoter:** POD Concerts **Website:** www.electricpicnic.ie

'Anything that makes Oxford University's Bodleian Library look short of info needs cash to keep going, so the more tickets and merchandise bought through the site the better'

Founded by Neil Greenway in 2000 and now owned and run by NRG Internet Ltd, eFestivals publishes an encyclopedic stash of event listings dating back to the year 2000. The focus is primarily on the UK scene with content spanning line-up, ticket price, location and date info, together with well-penned reviews, photos, exclusive interviews, video documentaries and even weather forecasts, all helping punters get a flavour before donning their wellies or bikinis. The site also tackles the challenges of festival-going – including sex and drugs – through honest, practical guides.

For a true picture of modern festival life just dip into its forums and blogs. You'll find reformation rumours (the Kinks?, The Stone Roses?), lonely souls looking for car shares ('Anyone up for Bloodstock?'), unfettered exuberance at line-up announcements ('EAT STATIC!!!… wicked!') and the pathos of humdrum lives ('…started my work today, dry goods at Waitrose').

Beyond the punter chat there's a solid industry backbone in the form of breaking news, noble promotion of lift-sharing schemes and a shop selling tickets and merchandise. Of course, anything that makes Oxford University's Bodleian Library look short of info needs cash to keep going, so the more tickets and merchandise bought through the site the better. Time to pull out that credit card. www.efestivals.co.uk

FUJI ROCK **FIELD DAY** FLEADH CHEOIL NA HÉIREANN

Now in its thirteenth year, the Fuji Rock Festival is set in probably the most stunning site in the world – the Naeba Ski Resort, Niigata, Japan. Surrounded by splendid forested mountains, with calf-strengthening woodland walks between stages, it's also the cleanest festival in the world. There's a receptacle for just about every kind of waste, from paper and bottles to discarded dreadlocks (OK, I made that one up). If you're a fan of Japanese cuisine you'll be in heaven; spotless cafés knock out hundreds of types of noodle, sushi and tempura. If you're tempted, book one of the local hotels in good time as they're in high demand, and if you're camping take your nine iron as the campsite's on a slightly hilly golf course and the rotters won't let you pitch a tent on the putting greens.

The first year of this legendary festival won't be forgotten by those who attended: a typhoon ripped through the site during the Red Hot Chili Peppers' set, although they carried on despite Anthony Kiedis having an already broken arm. Many ill-prepared Japanese suffered hypothermia so bad that they cancelled the second day, which turned out to be a beautiful sunny day with nary a breath of wind. Oh well.

From Lou Reed, Anthrax and Neil Young to Blur, Beck and the untouchable Tokyo Ska Paradise Orchestra – these acts represent just the tip of the iceberg in terms of acts played. I want to go – now!

FUJI ROCK

Location: Naeba, Japan **Founded:** 1997 **Current capacity:** 35,000 per day **Month:** July **Camping:** Yes **Nearest airports:** Narita/Haneda (Tokyo) **First headliners:** Green Day, Foo Fighters, The Prodigy, Red Hot Chili Peppers **Recent headliners:** Underworld, My Bloody Valentine, Primal Scream **Promoter:** Smash **Website:** www.fujirockfestival.com

orris dancing, a coconut shy, a tug of war and a wellie-throwing competition. Hardly the entertainment you'd expect to find at a cutting edge music all-dayer but just the sort of leftfield fun and games that make Field Day such an original festival experience. The brainchild of three of the most progressive club brands around, Field Day has been quick to carve a niche in a festival calendar fast becoming overrun with so-so events. Capacity is limited to just 5,000 in an area strewn with straw bales and sideshow attractions, ensuring an atmosphere more akin to that of an English village fête than a seething urine-splattered moshpit. The musical line-ups, meanwhile, are a hotbed of sideways electronica, art rock and Balearic wonderment, with the likes of Bat For Lashes, Andrew Weatherall and Richie Hawtin battling for your headspace over four stages, numerous tents and even the park bandstand.

One of the promoters, Tom Baker from Eat Your Own Ears, is also the prime mover behind east London's ambitious Concrete and Glass festival and once staged a tribute to Pink Floyd head loon Syd Barrett, so it's small surprise that Field Day is billed as a 'psychedelic summer fête'. As far as crazy diamonds go, this is one that's set to shine on for some time.

FIELD DAY

Location: Victoria Park, London, UK **Founded:** 2007 **Current capacity:** 5,000 **Month:** August **Camping:** No **Nearest airport:** Stansted **First headliners:** Justice, Four Tet, Erol Alkan **Recent headliners:** Foals, Mystery Jets, Simian Mobile Disco **Promoters:** Adventures In The Beetroot Field, Eat Your Own Ears and Bugged Out! **Website:** www.fielddayfestivals.com

f drowning gallons of Guinness and dancing like a loon were a sport, this event would be its Olympics. A peripatetic event held in the Irish Midlands' town of Tullamore since 2007, this fleadh (pronounced 'flah') is the largest celebration of Irish music, song and dance on the planet. The fiddle-di-do atmosphere seeps into every crevice; some 10,000 performers hit the town for concerts, street parades and workshops, forming a raucous walking cloud of flutes and fiddles, uilleann pipes, banjos and accordions. A quarter of a million revellers can be found in hot pursuit, powered by gallons of the black stuff and the craic.

Although the vibe is laissez-faire, there's a serious edge to the institution, originally founded to revive and set new standards in traditional Irish music through competition. More than 100 contests are held across town, with performers winning their place at these all-Ireland finals through regional battles. Record breaking also plays a key part; in 2008, an incredible 2,852 musicians, singers and dancers played en masse for 56 minutes, setting a world record for the biggest Irish music jam.

If the Celtic bug bites, you can always attend summer school music classes, open to even the most cloth-eared novice. Also, be aware that there are many contenders for the Fleadh crown, including Mean Fiddler's roving efforts held in the US, the UK and Australia.

FLEADH CHEOIL NA HÉIREANN

Location: Tullamore, County Offaly, Ireland **Founded:** 1951 **Current capacity:** 250,000+ **Month:** August **Camping:** Yes **Nearest airport:** Dublin **First headliner:** Thomas Street Pipers' Club **Recent headliners:** Innisfree Céilí Band, CCÉ, Fred Finn Branch, Sligeach **Promoter:** Comhaltas Ceoltóirí Éireann **Website:** www.fleadh2009.com

Om Shanti Shanti Shanti

GLASTONBURY GLOBAL GATHERING **GLADE** GREEN MAN GARDEN FESTIVAL

iniature fluffy puppets dancing in a strobelight. A man canoeing down a river of mud past a doughnut stall. The long slog to the Stone Circle at 5am. The 'poo train' toilet trailer leaving a crowd of people pinching their noses in its wake. Hay bales strewn across parched earth. Silk flags fluttering in the Jazz World field. The faraway roar of the crowd as another act finishes/the sun rises/someone falls flat on their face in the mud. The Penguin Café Orchestra locking down the free spirit of Glastonbury with their twirling strings and pulsating brass beats. Seeing a woven wristband dangling by a thread off a barman's arm in a dodgy pub in east London three months after the festival finished. Joe Strummer and Keith Allen drunkenly serenading the queue at the Joe Bananas blanket stall with a tiny boombox and red wine-stained gobs. Michael Eavis surrounded by hordes of journalists, updating them on the state of the flooded BBC compound. The beaming white teeth of a dreadlocked traveller covered from head to toe in dried mud. The sun rising over Glastonbury Tor.

Some of my favourite memories are from Glastonbury, which is strange as it's also the place where I'd expect to come away with the fewest memories due to the battering I've given my brain and body on the hallowed fields of Avalon. Glastonbury's been my favourite summer holiday for 17 years and no amount of mud, rain, sunburn, food poisoning or head-splitting pear-cider hangovers is going to stop me going till the day I die.

Glastonbury is the reason I'm writing this book and why I'm staging my own festival, Bestival. It's also mostly to blame for me starting a record label and bagging a show on Radio 1. It has completely saturated my life.

Fifteen years ago, I set off with my new girlfriend in my battered Citroen 2CV to travel from London to Glastonbury. I'd never been to a festival before and imagined a kind of village fête affair with rock bands instead of the brass bands I'd played the trombone in growing up. Ashamedly, I have to admit to jumping the fence; after parking the 2CV in one of the many farmers' driveways-turned-£5-car-parks, Josie and I crawled commando-style across field after field, blissfully unaware we could have just strolled up to the fence and handed over our £10 to use someone's ladder or hastily burrowed tunnel. We got shoved over the fence just in time to see Massive Attack take to the stage bathed in blue light, the bass booming out of the speakers like a subsonic submarine.

Later that weekend I watched The Orb in a daze, heard giant motorcycles roar in one ear and out the other, saw crusties and bankers dancing together in oblivion, gaped at fireworks shooting into the sky and caught a collective roar so loud it could be heard in Bristol. Lots of people hate camping but I love nothing more than trudging round in two feet of mud in a pair of shorts and some old trainers, watching random bands and eating veggie burgers from Manic Organic, all washed down with a pint of hot cider. Beautiful.

One of my favourite Glastonbury festivals was 2006 when, after a sun-kissed Wednesday and Thursday, the heavens opened on the Friday night. My wife Josie and I were staying in a friend's 'yurt', a sort of upside-down canvas and wood-framed fruitbowl. Suddenly, a month's worth of rain came down within the space of a few minutes. Our friends' tents next door were flooding and they sought refuge in our warm, dry yurt. Noticing the canvas chimney hole in the roof of our yurt bowing under the weight of a large puddle of water, I bounded out of bed in my birthday suit, went to push the puddle up and out from underneath only for the canvas to tear and a few gallons of water to soak me from head to foot. Shivering and halfway to pneumonia within a couple of hours, I couldn't have been happier as I sat in a friend's camper van sipping brandy coffee and laughing as half of Glastonbury floated off down the hill.

A few years before that, I proposed to Josie at Glastonbury. The romantic spot I chose was a patch of ground outside the Rizla tent strewn with discarded jacket potatoes and beer cans. Surrounded by loads of our friends, I dropped to one knee and dug out a ring I'd been hiding in my pocket for three nerve-racking days. Fittingly, DJ David Holmes dropped Primal Scream's 'Rocks' just at that moment. Josie thankfully said yes, we partied all night and before passing out I remember vomiting bright-green sick while laughing uproariously in the Stone Circle.

I wish I'd been at every Glastonbury festival since 1971 – two years before I was born – when the likes of Fairport Convention and David Bowie rubbed patchouli-scented shoulders with the likes of the Worthy Farm Windfuckers and Magic Muscle. In a video of the first festival, a dashing young Michael Eavis talks to camera while a white horse trots by in the background, a naked man with flowing locks astride the beast. Numerous hippies litter the background in various states of undress, passing around joints and flowers. It all looks like nirvana to my eyes.

Yes, things have moved on. I remember the uproar when the first cash machine turned up, when a mobile phone mast appeared and when the Fence of Doom was erected. But Glastonbury is a safer and better festival for it.

Other memories? Sat on the grass in front of the mighty Pyramid Stage as Rolf Harris rocks out. Dancing on the roof of a burnt-out jet plane in Trash City. Proof, if needed, that Glastonbury is the greatest show on earth.

GLASTONBURY

Location: Worthy Farm, Glastonbury, UK **Founded:** 1981 (previously Glastonbury Fayre from 1971) **Current capacity:** 134,000
Month: June **Camping:** Yes **Nearest airport:** Bristol **First headliners:** New Order, Hawkwind **Recent headliners:** Jay Z, Kings Of Leon,
The Verve **Promoters:** Glastonbury Festivals Ltd/Festival Republic **Website:** www.glastonburyfestivals.co.uk

didn't have a clue what I was doing the first year. It was 1970 and I'd been to the Bath Blues festival with my girlfriend. It was a mind-blowing experience for me; Flower Power was the mood of the moment, there were hippies everywhere and I got totally caught up in it. The music was terrific and I thought to myself 'let's set about it and do something on my farm'. I had no contacts so I phoned Colston Hall in Bristol to ask how to get in touch with the Kinks. I was playing 'Lola' to the cows at the time, on a makeshift sound system I'd set up in the milking parlour – I was wired up for music! I've always loved music and that's what's driven me.

Almost 40 years on we've just won International Festival of the Year for the fourth year running, so I must have got something right. I keep doing it because I love it, and people realise that we're here with a heart and soul. My family have been involved with this land since 1864, and people respect that and warm to the fact that this is our home. There's a feeling of safety, security and good politics that's carried throughout the festival I think.

We've had our share of trouble. I had to talk somebody down from throwing himself off a telegraph pole during the acid years. And it was heavy going in the late 1980s, when the travellers were coming at me from all sides. They were pretty scary and a lot of good people walked from the festival during that time. A convoy turned up from Nottingham once, looking for trouble, and I met them at the gates and gave them their own field to camp in. One of the traveller kids asked if I was Micheal Eavis and if she could have my autograph, which broke the ice a bit.

I never did get the Kinks that first year. We had Marc Bolan instead, and it's still one of the most inspiring performances I've ever seen. I think truly that moment is what gave me the nudge to keep going. Over the years I think people have learned from us and copied bits and pieces, but nobody will ever be able to deliver the whole thing like we do. We're still at the leading edge of the scene. We've become part of British history.

'Glastonbury is the greatest festival, the ongoing Woodstock' – Paul McCartney

'd met Paul McCartney years ago and asked him to play Glastonbury, but I knew it wouldn't happen until the time was right for him. Then one year his agent phoned up and asked for the Saturday night slot – but I already had Radiohead confirmed, and I told him he'd have to wait till next year. The agent said why didn't I call him back when I'd changed my mind, before 4pm if that was alright. Of course I didn't. Then the call came again early the following year, and I said fine – fantastic! In the end it went better than I could ever have imagined.

Steve Sutherland, who was editor of the *NME* at the time, said it was the best music concert of the last 50 years. Paul just fitted the festival so well. Everybody was in tears at the end of his set; it was very emotional. I went to see him right after – not before, I'd been told, he was too worked up – and he was thrilled, with big fat tears rolling down his cheeks. His set was brilliant and he played all the classics. 'Let It Be' and 'Michelle' went down especially well.

We went 15 minutes over the curfew, and Paul offered to pay the fine but I didn't take it off him. It was only £300. He put on such an amazing show, with fireworks that must have cost a bomb; he probably spent more on his set than I paid him as a fee. He said afterwards that he'd like to come back, and I'll take him up on it one day.

PAUL McCartney @ GLASTONBURY

Brilliant!

t started out as an excuse for 25,000 house and techno heads to party so hard that the only sound you heard at the end of the night was everyone on all fours scrabbling around trying to find their marbles. Today it's a bona fide 'proper' festival, with two days of big-name guests topping off a line-up that often reads like a who's who of dance music. Global Gathering is now a serious player in the UK, Europe and beyond, with a global reach that most competitors would give their right arms for. It is probably the only UK club brand that has managed to make (some) success of launching into North America.

Frankly, the venue – a disused airfield – is nothing to write home about but the organisers treat it as something of a blank canvas, sprinkling the set with fairground rides, chill out lounges, open air cinemas, hot air balloon trips and other diversionary entertainment. There are a myriad of stages and tents hosted by the likes of John Digweed's Bedrock label, their very own club Godskitchen and dance bible *Mixmag* to accommodate the heavy musical hitters. Historically, BBC Radio 1 have broadcast some of the event live.

The year 2008 represented a watershed year for the organisation, with parties being staged in Russia, Turkey, New Zealand, Malaysia, Australia, Poland, Ukraine and Belarus, following their initial international foray to the US in 2006. Global Gathering also bagged the Best British Festival gong at the 2008 *DJ Magazine* awards.

GLOBAL GATHERING

Location: Long Marston Airfield, nr Stratford Upon Avon, UK **Founded:** 2001 **Current capacity:** 55,000 **Month:** July **Camping:** Yes **Nearest airport:** Birmingham International **First headliners:** Judge Jules, David Morales, Roni Size **Recent headliners:** Kanye West, Mark Ronson, Sascha, Tiësto **Promoter:** Angel Music Group/MAMA Group **Website:** www.globalgathering.co.uk

The rave scene may have evolved since the days of bombing round the M25 while bawling into a CB radio, but it's good to see a slither of old-skool secrecy survives. The organisers of Glade, an electronic offshoot of the main Glastonbury showcase, are notoriously cagey about the event's location, detailing little more than 'somewhere in southern England' in their publicity material. What started as a well intentioned, if slightly ragged, affair in 2004 – overflowing toilets and somewhat dry bars were among the gripes – has evolved into a non-stop 12-arena bender of hip-hop, rave, techno, breakcore, jungle and ambient harvested from around the world. Even the chill out area has upped its game, offering quality organic grub and recharge-friendly tuneage. Big names are in abundance – Jeff Mills, The Orb, UNKLE, Dreadzone and Squarepusher have all performed – while unsung outfits such as A.Human (mashing prog, beats and grunge) and nascent knob-twiddler James Holden have dropped in some of the finest sets.

Despite the growth, the intimate vibe remains; blockbuster shows and aircraft hanger-sized tents are eschewed for smaller stages, real ale and proper camping (no segregation between stages and tents). The anti-corporate spirit remains intact too: you'll see sole traders and small outfits rather than fat-cat sponsors. As for finding the site, things will change in 2009, as the event will take place at Matterley Bowl home to the first ever Creamfields festival in 1998.

GLADE

Location: Matterley Bowl, Hampshire, UK **Founded:** 2004 **Current capacity:** 12,500 **Month:** July **Camping:** Yes **Nearest airport:** Heathrow
First headliners: Aphex Twin, Plump DJs **Recent headliners:** Jeff Mills, Pendulum **Promoter:** G Events **Website:** www.gladefestival.com

Like the best festivals, Green Man started out as a low-key gathering of a few hundred like-minded souls, built on friendship, quality music and good-time vibes. And even though it's snowballed into a modest 9,000-strong annual event, outgrowing two sites into the bargain, it still retains the inherent qualities from back in the day. As befitting a gathering held in the wilds of the Welsh hills – at a site described as the best in the country by *The Times* – Green Man taps into the Celtic atmosphere with an abundance of ceilidhs, midnight bonfires, storytelling and surprise gigs. Sure, the festival now spans four days and features big and small names across five stages, but there are plenty of tents devoted to folk music, DJing, theatre and literature. For those thinking more with their stomachs than their ears, there's lots of organic nosh and real ales on offer, a far cry from the slurry often served up at British festivals.

Like an increasing number of small-scale festivals, Green Man is family friendly; in fact, under-11s get in for free. Kids are well catered for and there's even a midwives tent dishing out advice on breastfeeding. The Green Field area is a particular highlight, featuring the Ringo Bingo music quiz, comedy performance, an eco fairground and the Solar Powered Milk Float Stage where people discuss environmental issues. Just don't mention the rain!

GREEN MAN

Location: Glanusk Park, Brecon, Wales, UK **Founded:** 2003 **Current capacity:** 10,000 **Month:** August **Camping:** Yes **Nearest airport:** Cardiff

First headliners: King Creosote, James Yorkston, The Memory Band **Recent headliners:** Spiritualized, Super Furry Animals, Pentangle

Promoters: Jo, Danny, Fi **Website:** www.thegreenmanfestival.co.uk

Croatia might not be the first place to spring to mind when looking for a slice of festival heaven, but The Garden Festival is fast changing perceptions of this eastern European country. The festival itself is set in the grounds of a traditional-style Croatian hotel near the seaside town of Zadar, taking over a small peninsula that grants lucky attendees stunning views of the surrounding coast and landscape. Indeed, the festival has also now expanded to two weekends in July, affording committed punters the opportunity to explore this beautiful section of the Adriatic coast in between the two main music sessions. Numbers are capped at 2,000 for each weekend in order to ensure a certain level of intimacy and freedom: A. N. Other enormo-festival this ain't.

Some of the UK's cooler club brands and DJs are now regular fixtures at The Garden Festival. The likes of Mr Scruff and Gilles Peterson ensure the sonic selection covers as many bases as possible while London clubs such as Secretsundaze and Mulletover host twice-daily, four-hour boat parties that meander up and down the coast, ferrying well-oiled punters between the festival site and Garden bar. Attendees of previous events are adamant that the period between about 4pm and sunset is the best time for partying – nothing beats dancing in the surf as the beats are cranked up.

THE GARDEN FESTIVAL

Location: The Garden Petrčane, Croatia **Founded:** 2006 **Current capacity:** 2,000 each weekend **Month:** July **Camping:** Yes **Nearest airports:** Zadar/Split/Zagreb **First headliners:** Mr Scruff, Rainer Trüby, Alice Russell **Recent headliners:** The Bays, Norman Jay, Crazy P **Promoters:** The Garden Zadar **Website:** www.thegardenfestival.eu

HIPPIES HOMEGAME HOVE

'If everyone had followed the mantra of 'never trust a hippy' most festivals today wouldn't even exist. Hippies could just see us through a gloomy world recession. Here's to the hippies!'

S melly, long-haired wastes of space? Or the purveyors of the original peace 'n' love vibrations that have made festivals tick since time began from Stonehenge to Woodstock? When the first hippie subculture kicked off in San Francisco's Haight Ashbury district and the Beat Generation started experimenting with psychedelic rock, even more psychedelic drugs and more often than not each others orifices, it didn't seem like this minority youth movement would burn so bright and last so long. In January 1967, the Human Be-In in Golden Gate Park lit the touchstone for the first Summer of Love. Two years later, as a warning rang out across the Woodstock site to 'not touch the brown acid' as a batch of dodgy LSD did the rounds, thousands of genuine, long-haired, dope smoking, sandal wearing, free love aficionados all turned to each other, swallowed a brown tab and floated downstream.

The movement later spread to the Mexican jipitecas, to New Zealand's nomadic housetruckers, to the peace convoys travelling around the world and the queues of rusty transit vans heading to Stonehenge. If everyone had followed the mantra of 'never trust a hippy' most music festivals today wouldn't even exist. Hippies helped turn us on to healthy eating, were responsible for the birth of the internet and led a lifestyle that could just see us through a gloomy world recession. So here's to the hippies!

As far as festivals go, Homegame must surely go down as one of the more intimate and unusual. With just a few hundred tickets for sale each year, performance spaces that accommodate just a handful of people and a musical policy that's so laid-back it's horizontal, Homegame is a quirky happening as far removed from your run-of-the-mill enormo-festival as it's possible to get. The event, promoted by the Fife-based Fence Records collective, takes place each year in a small fishing village called Anstruther, located deep in the bowels of the Scottish hinterlands. Homegame usually opens with 'a little soup and song' in the village hall – you purchase a bowl of soup and are then entertained by a number of acoustic performers. Throughout the weekend, bands play in pubs, school halls and assorted backrooms, with attendees strolling through the village from gig to gig. You might be asked to carry things around – this is a real do-it-yourself festival – and bands often borrow leads, drums and equipment from each other. It all helps give the festival its unique air.

Music-wise, you can expect the likes of King Creosote, Kieran Hebden, The Earlies, Lone Pigeon and Pictish Trail and after parties (sometimes in a room above the church hall) are legendary, fuelled by acoustic guitars, red wine and a whole lot of love, ensuring Homegame feels like the best house party ever.

HOMEGAME

Location: Anstruther, Scotland, UK **Founded:** 2004 **Current capacity:** 300 **Month:** April **Camping:** No **Nearest airport:** Edinburgh
First headliner: King Creosote **Recent headliner:** The Pictish Trail **Promoter:** Fence Records **Website:** www.fencerecords.com

magine your fantasy five-day session. Remote island with pristine beaches and woods? Check. Beautiful people? Check. Eclectic international acts, installation art and literature. Check. In fact, this Norwegian gathering even scores on the green front, billed as Scandinavia's first carbon-neutral festival. I had the pleasure of playing the first Hove. After a beautiful boat ride skippered by a drunk Captain Birdseye lookalike, it started raining. And didn't stop for four days. But that didn't stop me loving the whole back-to-nature Viking vibe and me or Fred from Lemon Jelly DJing a set that swung from doo wop to gabba … oh yeah, and you may need a wheelbarrow of cash for a round of beers.

As for tunes, the event dilutes heavy doses of goth, metal and prog rock with blues, electro and outfits that simply defy categorisation: the UK's Chrome Hoof, for example, melded hip-hop and metal with jazz, disco and house in 2008. And alongside international names such as the Kaiser Chiefs, Amy Winehouse and The Long Blondes stand home-grown talents such as unrepentant krautrockers 120 Days and the theatrical Animal Alpha.

Civilised guesthouses are available while campsites give you the choice of bedding down on-site, kipping on a quieter ground ten minutes away or lounging on the shoreline. Not that you'll be spending much time under canvas; the Nordic summer will treat you to two hours of darkness a night. A great excuse to stay up forever!

HOVE FESTIVAL

Location: Hove, Tromøy, Norway **Founded:** 2007 **Current capacity:** 20,000 **Month:** June **Camping:** Yes **Nearest airports:** Oslo, Kjevik (Kristiansand)/Torp (Sandefjord) **First headliner:** Queens Of The Stone Age **Recent headliners:** The Gossip, The Killers, Slayer **Promoter:** Renaissance (2007) **Website:** www.hovefestival.com

ISLE OF WIGHT I LOVE TECHNO

Isle of Wight
Festival of Music
Saturday august 30th 1969

Nº 53926

BOB DYLAN
and
THE BAND
THE WHO
RICHIE HAVENS
TOM PAXTON
MOODY BLUES
JOE COCKER
FAT MATTRESS

NR RYDE IOW
FIERY CREATIONS LTD.

£2

A few miles from our house on the Isle of Wight is a picturesque patchwork of hills, dales and cliffs overlooking the sea. I often drive my old put-putting yellow camper van there and look out over the fields, imagining the gargantuan sea of people that had amassed there in 1970. East Afton Farm, the site for the 1970 Isle of Wight festival, was the event's final resting place after two smaller events in 68 (10,000 people) and 69 (150,000) elsewhere on the island. With more folk turning up in 1970 than had even gone to Woodstock, people still talk about this as one of the largest ever gatherings of human beings to have taken place. Estimates range from 600,000 upwards; bearing in mind that the Isle Of Wight has a permanent population of just over 150,000, it's a surprise the whole bloody island didn't tip over and dunk everyone in the drink.

Anyway, back to 1970. It all started on Wednesday, a measly three pounds to get in and a 300-acre campsite and 38-acre grass arena for ticket holders. Unfortunately, boatloads of Spanish, French and Italian anarchists had pitched up in readiness for a free gig and the organisers had to bribe them with free Mars bars – yes Mars bars – not to break in. Sadly, some molten chocolate didn't prove sufficient currency to stop around half a million people tearing down fences, pissing everywhere (despite the half a mile of urinals on offer) and generally having a right old laugh at the organisers' expense.

Band wise it was a veritable who's who of 60s rock royalty. Kris Kristofferson, Procul Harum, Supertramp and the like warmed proceedings up before The Doors, Joni Mitchell, Sly and The Family Stone and The Who royally smashed it up. The festival culminated with a now-legendary performance from Jimi Hendrix who came onto the stage around midnight looking a bit out of sorts and played a mangled version of 'God Save The Queen' while someone set fire to the stage. Three weeks later Jimi was found dead and the 60s were disappearing up in a cloud of smoke.

And if you don't really feel I've done it justice, watch the amazing documentary with hilarious footage of the promoters knee-deep in old banknotes, crazy hippy types wandering around and ill-prepared promoter Rikki Farr boasting, 'The new site will cover 300 acres and is set up in such a way as to provide people with an entire self-contained community, without infringing on the rights of local inhabitants' just before half of Europe chipped up and smashed his back door in.

I wish I'd been there as I still think it must have been one of the most exciting gatherings to have ever gone down. Local resident TP Kelsey put it best: 'The festival provided an alternative society. A society where people forgot their own particular class, creed, race or religion and were able to live together and do the simple things of life on a friendly basis.'

ISLE OF WIGHT – THE ORIGINAL

Location: East Afton Farm, Freshwater, Isle of Wight, UK **Founded:** 1968 **Capacity:** 600,000 **Month:** August **Camping:** Yes **Nearest airports:** Bembridge/Southampton **1968 headliners:** Jefferson Airplane, T.Rex, The Crazy World Of Arthur Brown **1970 headliners:** The Who, The Doors, Jimi Hendrix, Leonard Cohen **Promoter:** Fiery Creations **Website:** www.isleofwightfestival.com

Revived in 2002 by the Isle of Wight council and then taken on by live agent John Giddings and his Solo agency, the Isle of Wight festival carries on the good work laid down by the original festies back in the day, namely bringing mammoth acts to the island. From The Rolling Stones and David Bowie to Muse, Coldplay and The Police, the new festival has real pulling power and is now very much giving the big boys of Glastonbury, Reading and V a serious run for their money. Taking place in Seaclose Park in the middle of Newport, the capital of the Isle of Wight, the site is a buzzing hive of fairground rides, smaller musical stages and a giant main stage where so many legends have performed. There's even the beautiful River Medina running alongside it. Much has been made of a rivalry between the Isle of Wight festival and our own Bestival, but this is just gossip cooked up for a good story. The reality is that the Isle of Wight now has two award-winning, world-famous but very different festivals which have brought acts as diverse as The Who and REM to My Bloody Valentine and Aphex Twin to a small island nestled off the south coast of the UK. Wight on!

ISLE OF WIGHT – NEW

Location: Seaclose Park, Newport, Isle of Wight **Founded:** 2002 **Current capacity:** 70,000 **Month:** June **Camping:** Yes **Nearest airports:** Bembridge/Southampton **First headliners:** Robert Plant, The Charlatans, Starsailor **Recent headliners:** The Prodigy, Basement Jaxx, The Police **Promoter:** Solo **Website:** www.isleofwightfestival.com

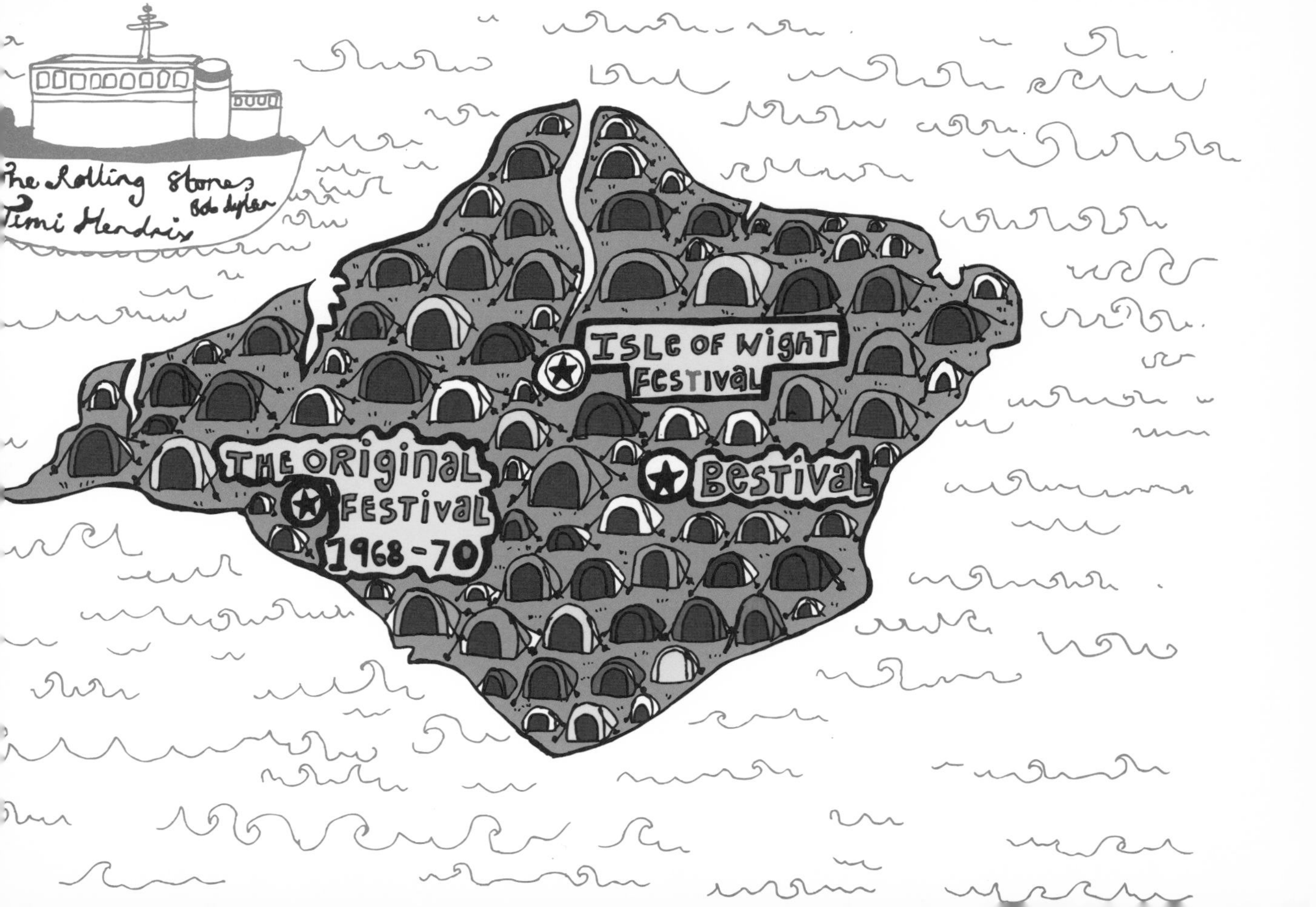

The Rolling Stones
Jimi Hendrix
Bob Dylan

ISLE OF WIGHT FESTIVAL

THE ORIGINAL FESTIVAL 1968-70

BESTIVAL

Love Techno is one of those does-what-it-says-on the-tin festivals. That's not a slight, merely an observation that if you like your beats that little bit harder then this is the festival for you. Ever since 1995 – when the inaugural festival attracted a mere 700 souls – I Love Techno has attracted the biggest players from the techno scene, serving up wickedly fierce rhythms for a crowd that loves to party hard. Well hard, in fact. You might think that the venue – Expo centres are usually home to conferences and trade fairs – would make for a sterile partying environment. You'd be wrong. The best thing is that there's none of that tedious traipsing through mud, no getting lost in a sea of identikit tents and rarely a queue for the toilet. There are hundreds of armchairs and settees scattered around for chilling, colour-coded rooms and clever signposting, a room housing professional photographers and make-up artists and a general top-notch approach to organisation. After all, we're here to enjoy ourselves, not take part in Battle of the Somme-style trench warfare.

British techno icon Dave Clarke has been a mainstay of I Love Techno, featuring on the bill most years since the festival's inception, while the likes of Richie Hawtin, Underworld, DJ Rush, Ben Sims, Marco Bailey, Adam Beyer and others have ensured there's never been a let-up in either pace or musical fury.

I LOVE TECHNO

Location: Flanders Expo, Gent, Belgium **Founded:** 1995 **Current capacity:** 35,000 **Month:** October **Camping:** No **Nearest airport:** Brussels
First headliners: Daft Punk, Richie Hawtin, Jeff Mills **Recent headliners:** Underworld, Boys Noize, Richie Hawtin **Promoter:** Live Nation
Website: www.ilovetechno.be

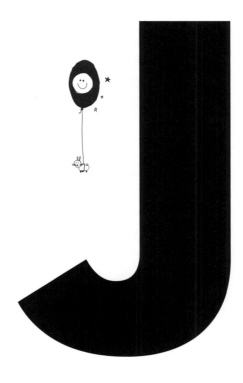

JIMI / JANIS / JONI

'Ravi Shankar was on the sitar, Janis Joplin was on the bourbon and Jimi Hendrix took a shine to a can of lighter fuel, setting fire to his guitar to create one of the most iconic moments in rock history'

Naked bodies writhing in the mud; blissed-out beardies with flowers in their hair; guitarists with headbands impregnated with LSD. Psychedelic high jinks are as embedded in our festival DNA as mud and whiffy toilets. Wordsmiths laid down the psychedelic movement's foundations in 1950s, with Beat writers such as Jack Kerouac and Aldous Huxley seeking enlightenment (or just enough inspiration to finish a novel) by dabbling in mescaline, benzedrine and – the real heavyweight – LSD. Before long, even arch-squares The Beach Boys were donning flowery shirts and attempting to emulate the effects of mind-altering drugs, experimenting with feedback, stream-of-consciousness babbling, chanting, crazy time changes and, God help us, improvised celery-crunching.

Just as California was building up a psychedelic head of steam with the likes of Janis Joplin's soulful *Cheap Thrills*, UK bands The Beatles and Pink Floyd fought back with seminal albums *Sgt Pepper's Lonely Hearts Club Band* and *The Piper At The Gates Of Dawn*. Even the Rolling Stones, until 1966 a spiky rhythm'n' blues band, attempted to board the magic bus with *Their Satanic Majesties Request*, dismissed by many as a low-budget psychedelia clone.

If you had a time machine, you'd set your coordinates for three key trips. First up, a stroll around San Francisco's Haight-Ashbury district in the mid 60s, a hotbed of counter culture where it was impossible to step more than a few yards in your purple flares without bumping into Allen Ginsberg and members of the Grateful Dead.

Next up would be California's 1967 Monterey Pop Festival. With a bill featuring the Mamas And The Papas and Scott Mackenzie, the event set the template for the modern rock fest. Ravi Shankar was on the sitar, Janis Joplin was on the bourbon and Jimi Hendrix took a shine to a can of lighter fuel, setting fire to his guitar to create one of the most iconic moments in rock history.

Your final stop is August 1970, the Isle of Wight; for many, psychedelia's spectacular nadir and swansong rolled into one. The Doors, Donovan, T. Rex and Joni Mitchell all played while Jimi Hendrix, not long for this world, bled distortion and feedback from every pore. The stage caught fire at the close of his set. The combustible psychedelic 60s had finally gone up in smoke.

Of course the movement lives on, even if the Mandelbrot graphics and droopy moustaches are long gone. Not bad for a chance concoction in Switzerland in 1943, when scientist Albert Hofmann synthesized a compound and accidentally experienced the world's first acid trip while cycling home.

K

KIDS KNEBWORTH

Kids, who'd have 'em? Well, we would actually, and probably so would a lot of you. Many folk see festivals and kids going together like sand and glue and it's true that the moshpit for Rage Against The Machine at Reading or a baby in a bassbin at Creamfields is no place for young 'uns. However, while some perennially family-friendly festivals – Guildford, Glastonbury and WOMAD in particular – have always accommodated the nappy crew, more and more festivals are waking up to the fact that not only do more kids mean more parents coming, but the children are also future festival goers themselves. Snare them in now and they'll never leave. Ah hah hah hah (that's my evil laugh!). Cynicism aside it's a massive relief as a parent to encounter crews such as Happy Crappers who provide clean, lockable toilets for families, responsible festivals like The Big Chill and Green Man who have very good family campsites and stewards who 'tag' children with their names and parents' phone numbers for when they wander off to see Iggle Piggle and end up watching Iggy Pop.

For the pure kids' vibe and no adult numpties to spoil the fun, check out Glastonbury Children's Festival and Bristol Children's Festival (both in August), the Mega Mela in Manchester and (here comes a shameless plug!) our very own Camp Bestival. It's designed specifically for families and boasts more than 100 free things for kids to do, from meeting Angelina Ballerina and learning to DJ to listening to Howard Marks read bedtime stories sat on the side of the stage. And not a reefer in sight!

HAZEL
FRANKIE
HARLAND
INDIE
CHERRY
MERLIN
ARLO + PIP

Awight Knob-Worth?!' yelled Mick Jagger in 1976, setting the tone for three decades of rock histrionics in a field. Knebworth, an ancestral home dating back as far as the Domesday Book, practically invented the moshing/magic mushroom/flying-bottles-of-piss festival formula, propelling the likes of Led Zeppelin and Queen into rock aristocracy. A few skirmishes with the authorities in the 1970s – neighbours complained about the din from more than seven miles away – led to some barmy bill tinkering (Cliff Richard anyone?) before the power-chord wagon was firmly put back on the rails by the likes of Meat Loaf and Deep Purple. Britpop rockers Oasis set the bar even higher in 1996 with two gigs over one balmy August weekend – more than 250,000 lucky punters witnessed Noel and co, after an incredible three million people applied for tickets (that's one in 20 of the UK population). Incredibly, Robbie Williams managed to top that in August 2003, as Knebworth hosted the biggest music event in British history – the former Take That-er performed to 375,000 people over three days. With sporadic events since then, we can only hope that, to quote Sir Mick, this institution doesn't fade away.

KNEBWORTH

Location: Knebworth, Hertfordshire, UK **Founded:** 1974 **Current capacity:** 125,000 **Month:** August **Camping:** No **Nearest airport:** Luton
First headliner: Allman Brothers **Recent headliners:** Robbie Williams, Underworld, 2ManyDJs **Website:** www.knebworthhouse.com

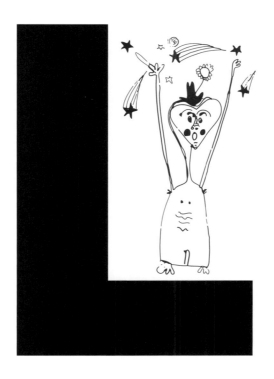

LOLLAPALOOZA LAKE OF STARS MALAWI MUSIC FESTIVAL LATITUDE
LOST VAGUENESS LOVEBOX WEEKENDER LARMER TREE FESTIVAL

Conceived by Jane's Addiction singer Perry Farrell, Lollapalooza has enjoyed rollercoaster fortunes since its inception in 1991. Pitched as a cross between a music gig, circus freakshow and consciousness-raising experience, the travelling festival toured venues throughout the US during its first six years of existence and helped give massive breaks to the likes of the Smashing Pumpkins and Nine Inch Nails. After a six-year hiatus – due in part both to the withdrawal of Farrell's involvement and the decline in popularity of alternative rock – Lollapalooza was resurrected as an annual weekend festival in Grant Park, Chicago, where it continues to this day.

The early years featured grunge stalwarts such as Soundgarden and Pearl Jam although often threw in hip-hop curveballs like Ice-T and Arrested Development. Lollapalooza also tapped into the prevailing early-90s counterculture mood, with tents hosting provocative art, non-profit organisations promoting their causes and the Jim Rose Circus Sideshow bringing a welcome slice of Victorian-style freakshowism. Metallica and The Prodigy headed up the bills in the late 90s before the festival ran out of steam. But now its bigger and better than ever.

In case you are wondering, 'Lollapalooza' is early twentieth century American slang for 'wonderful person or thing'. It also refers to a 'large lollipop', a more accurate description of the event.

LOLLAPALOOZA

Location: Grant Park, Chicago, USA **Founded:** 1991 **Current capacity:** 65,000 **Month:** August **Camping:** No **Nearest airport:** Chicago O'Hare
First headliners: Ice-T, Nine Inch Nails, Jane's Addiction **Recent headliners:** Radiohead, Rage Against The Machine, Kanye West **Promoters:** C3 Presents, Perry Farrell and The William Morris Agency **Website:** www.lollapalooza.com

August 7-9, 2009 Grant Park, Chicago

Lake Of Stars is something of a labour of love for promoter Will Jameson, who first visited Malawi in 1998 when working as a volunteer for the Wildlife Society. Upon his return to the UK, he started a club night in Liverpool called Chibuku Shake Shake – named after a Malawian beer - before going back to Malawi to stage the first Lake Of Stars festival, an event headlined by Chibuku regular Andy Cato from Groove Armada. (Incidentally, Cato took nearly three days to reach the festival site, thanks to a string of cancelled flights, but dropped a classic DJ set next to a performance from Malawian reggae kingpins the Black Missionaries.) The festival has blossomed ever since and is now a showcase for international dance music DJs and local African music talent, boosts the local economy to the tune of some £100,000 a year and places the region firmly on the global festival map.

For many, getting there is half the fun; each year more and more attendees embark on a pre-festival road trip, starting from Johannesburg and taking in some of southern Africa's most stunning landscapes. The destination ain't bad either – Lake Malawi is little short of a sun-kissed paradise. And with profits from the event going directly to charities operating in the local area – such as the Microloan Foundation and UNICEF – you can party hard with your conscience intact.

LAKE OF STARS MALAWI MUSIC FESTIVAL

Location: Sunbird Livingstonia Beach Hotel, Senga Bay, Lake Malawi, Malawi **Founded:** 2004 **Current capacity:** 3,000 **Month:** October **Camping:** Yes **Nearest airport:** Lilongwe **First headliner:** Andy Cato (Groove Armada) **Recent headliners:** Scratch Perverts, Mary Anne Hobbs, DJ Skitz **Promoter:** Will Jameson **Website:** www.lakeofstars.org

A lthough a relative newcomer to the UK scene, Latitude is backed by the might of Festival Republic, the organisation powering the Leeds, Reading and Glastonbury shindigs. Latitude's selling point is an emphasis on arts and creativity, in addition to an impressive range of first-rate pop, folk and indie bands. Latitude is packed with theatre, film, poetry, comedy and literature events, making full use of its idyllic setting. Green credentials are also there for all to see – solar powered showers, composting toilets, organic food, deposits for your beer glasses – and the general air is genteel and refined, like Hay-on-Wye with guitars. DJing on a tiny sound system in the woods at the first festival was both surreal and cosy as most of the festi goers had gone to bed by midnight!

Other highlights include comedian Ross Noble taking audience participation one step further as he led several hundred people on a conga around the campsite following his headlining stand-up set. Later that weekend, a man played a flute inside a giant bubble floating on the central lake while a burlesque dancer was suspended (painfully) from a tree by hooks in her skin. Latitude thrives on its widescreen line-ups – few competitors would offer up harmonica king Eli Reed, post-hardcore legends The Mars Volta and surreal comedy genius Bill Bailey on the same bill – and looks destined to set up camp in the leftfield for many more years to come.

LATITUDE

Location: Henham Park, Southwold, Suffolk, UK **Founded:** 2006 **Current capacity:** 25,000 **Month:** July **Camping:** Yes **Nearest airport:** Norwich **First headliners:** Snow Patrol, Antony & The Johnsons, Mogwai **Recent headliners:** Franz Ferdinand, Sigur Rós, Interpol **Promoter:** Festival Republic **Website:** www.latitudefestival.co.uk

'Once the main acts have left the stage and the Glasters crazy juice has kicked in, it seems all roads point towards Lost Vagueness no matter who you are or where you are on the site'

've lost count of the number of times I've stumbled along the disused railway line at Glastonbury in the wee hours of the morning looking for fun and games. Once the main acts have left the stage and the Glasters crazy juice has kicked in, it seems all roads point towards Lost Vagueness no matter who you are or where you are on the site. Turn the corner into the Vagueness field and what comes into view are the Ballroom, the Diner (complete with aeroplane nose cone top table) and the fantastic Dressing Up tent. The feeling of excitement mingled with a few drops of fear and trepidation is overwhelming. A dreadlocked crusty revs up a mutant motorbike with giant flaming wheels; a metallic horse clanks across a field breathing fire; a heavily pierced punk girl wheelspins a mini pink tank around in circles; a vast temporary steel shed erected days earlier hosts a boxing ring with two lesbian wrestlers greased up and scratching each other's faces; and the hammering sound of gabba mixed with scratchy old rock'n'roll echoes across the whole magical scene.

Sadly, after two decades of stressing out Health and Safety officers – thanks to a cocktail of laughter, laughing gas and more pyrotechnics than bonfire night in Bombay – Lost Vagueness has parted company with Glastonbury and moved onto pastures new. They remain, however, the godfathers of the 24-hour party people mindset.

LOVEBOX WEEKENDER

Location: Victoria Park, London, UK **Founded:** 2001 **Current capacity:** 25,000 **Month:** July **Camping:** No **Nearest airport:** Stansted

First headliner: Groove Armada **Recent headliners:** Flaming Lips, Goldfrapp **Promoters:** Lovebox/Mama Group **Website:** www.lovebox.net

Although the Lovebox Weekender only started in 2001, it feels like it's been around London's growing day festival scene forever. The brainchild of chart-topping dance act Groove Armada, the three-day bash is more colourful and innovative than most inner city festies and even a ludicrously early finish time doesn't stop the party people raving away. Reggae, indie, funk and soul acts have been added in latter years and the event grabbed the Best Medium-Sized Festival gong at the 2008 UK Festival Awards, the Oscars of the UK festival industry.

LARMER TREE FESTIVAL

Location: Larmer Tree Gardens, Salisbury, UK **Founded:** 1990 **Current capacity:** 4,000 **Month:** July **Camping:** Yes **Nearest airport:** Bournemouth **First headliner:** DHSS **Recent headliner:** Jools Holland **Promoter:** J&J Events **Website:** www.larmertreefestival.co.uk

Now this is a little gem of a five-day shindig. Small on numbers, big on woolly jumpers and not a nasty corporate sponsor in sight. The Midsummer Night's Dream setting – General Pitt Rivers' restored Victorian gardens with lawns, woodland, ponds and pavilion tea room – only adds to the bucolic charm. The bill spans acoustic and world outfits such as The Waterboys alongside decent jazz, blues and reggae turns. And beyond the stages are kids' activities – the event bagged the Family Festival Award 2008 – along with open-mic spots, street theatre, workshops (the Knitting Noras hosted a mean crochet session), holistic therapies and interviews conducted by media moguls such as Mark Kermode. Book well in advance.

MUD MOVEMENT: DETROIT'S ELECTRONIC MUSIC FESTIVAL
MELTDOWN MONTREUX JAZZ FESTIVAL

'Before the days of E.coli, it was almost a rite of passage to dive headfirst into the mud at WOMAD or Reading but these days there are far too many namby pamby health and safety scares and the mud folk seem in danger of extinction'

Mud, mud, glorious, sodding, dirty, sticky, stinking, trainer-destroying, wheel-spinning, slippy, slidey, oops there I go again on my bloody bruised arse mud. As a young reveller at festivals in my formative years, I thought nothing of spending the weekend covered in mud from the soles of my Doc Marten boots to the tip of my stupid magic mushroom hat. Now, as I gingerly step my suede loafers between rivers of the brown stuff at festivals from Somerset to Sydney (yes, we once got caught in such a tropical deluge of rain that even the Aussie soil turned into a red sludge), I sometimes wish I was indoors watching it on the telly. Before the days of E.coli, it was almost a rite of passage to dive headfirst into the mud at WOMAD or Reading but these days there are far too many namby pamby health and safety scares and the mud folk seem in danger of extinction.

If you're feeling browned off that there's not enough mud fun left at festivals, then head to the National Wetlands Centre in Llanelli in September as crowds gather for the National Mud Festival of Wales. It includes such downright dirty sports as wellie wanging and a tug of war also known as the Mud of War (see what they've done there?!) and also the chance to make a mud hut and eat edible mud pies. It's muddy marvellous but I'll stick to Glastonbury, thanks.

Detroit was always the logical location for a mass celebration of electronic music culture. As the birthplace of techno, the Motor City has churned out more top-draw DJs, producers and record labels than almost anywhere else. And thanks to killer line-ups and a jaw-dropping location, the Detroit Electronic Music Festival (DEMF) was destined to be a success from day one. Techno mainman Carl Craig was appointed musical director of the first DEMF in 2000. Thanks in part to free entry, the event reportedly attracted more than one million visitors to the city's downtown Hart Plaza and was heralded as an unqualified success. Hearing the likes of techno demigods Kevin Saunderson, Richie Hawtin and Craig himself spin and perform stone-cold classics right in the centre of the city that spawned them was, for many in the scene, a long-overdue recognition of the impact of electronic music both locally and globally.

Although Craig parted company with DEMF in advance of the 2001 festival, subsequent years have maintained the momentum of the inaugural event, with techno icons Derrick May and Kevin Saunderson each taking turns helming proceedings. It may have undergone a series of name changes and is now a ticket-only affair but the continuing quality of talent on show cannot be disputed; even mysterious techno recluse Moodymann was tempted to perform in 2008. Interestingly, May has exported the Movement concept to Italy, with the third edition in 2008 attracting more than 10,000 techno heads. *Ottimo*!

MOVEMENT: DETROIT'S ELECTRONIC MUSIC FESTIVAL

Location: Detroit, USA **Founded:** 2000 **Current capacity:** 75,000 **Month:** May **Camping:** No **Nearest airport:** Detroit **First headliners:** Richie Hawtin, Carl Craig, Kevin Saunderson **Recent headliners:** Moodymann, Josh Wink, Derrick May **Promoter:** Paxahau **Website:** www.demf.com

As far as city-based music festivals go, Meltdown's cultural aims are ambitious and lofty. And – thanks to a key selling point that sees a different music industry figure curate the line-up each year – you're guaranteed not to get the same-old same-old. The first Meltdown festival in 1993 was headed up by composer George Benjamin and featured classical music kingpins such as conductor Markus Stenz, the London Sinfonietta and soprano Sarah Stowe. Later years have seen a shift to more contemporary line-ups, with the likes of David Bowie, Jarvis Cocker, Scott Walker, Lee 'Scratch' Perry and the late John Peel taking turns in the musical director hot-seat. In 2008, trip-hop legends Massive Attack were the first band to take charge of the festival.

Standout performances have been legion, including original hard rockers Motörhead blasting eardrums and speakers at the Royal Festival Hall; Pete Doherty singing Disney songs; the Balanescu Quartet covering Jimi Hendrix's 'Foxy Lady'; and avant-garde Austrian rockers Fuckhead stripping naked and shoving washing-line cord up their bottoms.

Held over nine days in a string of venues overlooking the river Thames, including the Southbank Centre, Queen Elizabeth Hall and Royal Festival Hall, Meltdown also includes a comprehensive programme of talks, film screenings and artistic performance.

MELTDOWN

Location: Southbank Centre **Founded:** 1993 **Current capacity:** Various **Month:** June **Camping:** No **Nearest airport:** Gatwick

First headliner: George Benjamin **Recent headliners:** Massive Attack, Gong, YMO **Website:** www.southbankcentre.co.uk/meltdown

The Chemical Brothers, Gnarls Barkley and, er, Velvet Revolver... hang on, this looks as much like a jazz line-up as a chocolate cuckoo clock. Despite playing host to every noodle-monger going – Miles Davis and Ella Fitzgerald among them – Claude Nobs's legendary event has long-since tempered the atonal brew with long draughts of blues, soul, dance, rock and rap. The early 1970s are largely to blame. The festival's inaugural venue, the Montreux Casino, burned down in 1971 in true rock'n'roll style during a Frank Zappa set (an overzealous fan fired a flare gun) and soon Pink Floyd, Deep Purple and Led Zep were crawling all over the institution like a leather-trousered millipede.

Today, however, such splicing is surprisingly successful, even if the venue is now a rather less salubrious conference centre. Punters can bounce between myriad stages to sample good-time swingsters such as A Few Good Men or filter-disco kings Round Table Knights. Purists, meanwhile, can still spend the entire 16 days locked in the equivalent of a jazz cupboard by sticking to trad venues such as Casino Barrière.

If in doubt, spend some time outdoors. There are scores of free gigs around the picturesque town and the setting is one of the best on the festival circuit, perched on the banks of Lake Geneva in the shadow of the Alps.

MONTREUX JAZZ FESTIVAL

Location: Montreux, Switzerland **Founded:** 1967 **Current capacity:** 14,000 (230,00 across the event) **Month:** July **Camping:** No **Nearest airport:** Geneva International **First headliners:** Charles Lloyd, Keith Jarrett, Cecil McBee, Jack DeJohnette **Recent headliners:** Norah Jones, Prince, Faithless **Promoter:** Montreux Jazz Festival Foundation **Website:** www.montreuxjazz.com

NOTTING HILL CARNIVAL
NEW ORLEANS JAZZ & HERITAGE FESTIVAL

Europe's largest street festival smashes every record in the book. Founded as a celebration of Afro-Caribbean culture attracting just 500 people, it's now a full-on three-dayer cramming the streets of west London with hundreds of thousands of revellers, quaking sound systems, steaming piles of jerk cuisine, steel bands, more than 100 floats and booty-shaking of the highest order. Around 10,000 litres of Jamaican stout, 25,000 bottles of rum and five tons of chicken were consumed in 2008, while a fat £100 million was estimated to be generated for London's economy. When you go, be prepared for some of the most frantic hours of your life. You'll be assailed by hip-hop and reggae sound systems at every turn, while the main 3.5-mile procession, held on the final day, is an eye-popping sartorial riot: mass bands form phalanxes of bright orange plumes, leopard skin, glittering beaded bikinis, pharaohs and even erotic, er, cows.

The event was founded on noble ideals too. In contrast to today's upmarket enclave, the Notting Hill of the late 1950s was a downtrodden quarter, its boarding houses greeting newly arrived Caribbean immigrants with 'no blacks, no Irish, no dogs' signs. Race riots ensued and the carnival was established in an attempt to heal the racial rifts. Today, with every country in attendance from Afghanistan to the Philippines, it's doing a sterling job.

NOTTING HILL CARNIVAL

Location: Notting Hill, London, UK **Founded:** 1964 **Current capacity:** 2.5 million+ **Month:** August **Camping:** No **Nearest airports:** Heathrow/Gatwick **Promoter:** LNHC Ltd **Website:** www.nottinghillcarnival.biz

New Orleans may have suffered more than most in recent years but, hurricane or no hurricane, you can be assured that the music will never stop flowing. Approaching the end of its fourth decade in business, the Jazz Fest (as it's known locally) celebrates New Orleans' and Louisiana's rich history of music and culture. As well as blues, jazz and R'n'B, styles such as zydeco, bluegrass, Afro-Caribbean and Cajun music are all given airtime at a festival that's a riot of colour, sound and imagination. It's second only to the city's Mardi Gras in terms of pulling power for tourists.

Held on a large horse racing track about ten minutes from the vibrant and fashionable French Quarter, the usual set-up is around a dozen main stages for music, with a host of smaller stalls selling local arts and crafts and indigenous Louisiana cuisine, such as crawfish and alligator. In 2001 – the centenary of the birth of jazz legend Louis Armstrong – a mammoth 650,000 people attended the festival, including 160,000 on one day. With a widescreen music vision that has seen disparate entertainers such as Miles Davis, Erykah Badu, LL Cool J and Bob Dylan all grace the stages, the Jazz Fest shows few signs of letting up, no matter what the elements throw at it.

NEW ORLEANS JAZZ & HERITAGE FESTIVAL

Location: Fair Grounds Race Course, New Orleans, USA **Founded:** 1970 **Current capacity:** 400,000 **Month:** April **Camping:** No **Nearest airport:** New Orleans **First headliner:** Mahalia Jackson **Recent headliners:** Stevie Wonder, Sheryl Crow, Robert Plant **Promoter:** New Orleans Jazz & Heritage Festival & Foundation **Website:** www.nojazzfest.com

OZZFEST OXEGEN

t's unclear what's more remarkable: that Ozzy Osbourne is still living the rock'n'roll dream or that he's even still alive. Given the abuse he has subjected his body to during nearly 40 years of musical mayhem, it's a near miracle that Ozzy is able to stand up straight, let alone promote and headline a touring heavy-metal festival that bears his name and spirit. It all started in 1996 when the Black Sabbath frontman wasn't allowed into the Lollapalooza festival. So he staged his own Ozzfest, an event so successful that it become an annual happening, expanded to the UK and continental Europe and was even the subject of a reality TV show (*Battle For Ozzfest*, where the winning band bagged a festival slot. The show made a star of wife Sharon long before *X-Factor*). The tour usually attracts metal and thrash heavyweights – hello Metallica, Slayer, System Of A Down – and more often than not features Ozzy in the headline slot. (A reformed Black Sabbath headlined in 2004/5.)

It's not all been smooth sailing though. When Queens Of The Stone Age singer Josh Homme – whose band appeared at a free version of Ozzfest in 2007 – slated the event, Ozzy's wife Sharon reportedly responded in typically blunt fashion: 'I hope he gets syphilis and dies. I hope his dick fuckin' falls off so his mother can eat it.' The 2008 Ozzfest was a one-off show in Texas, and plans to resurrect the format have yet to be finalised.

OZZFEST

Location: Pizza Hut Park, Frisco, Texas, USA **Founded:** 1996 **Current capacity:** 50,000 **Month:** August **Camping:** No **Nearest airport:** Dallas
First headliners: Ozzy Osbourne, Slayer **Recent headliners:** Ozzy Osbourne, Metallica **Promoter:** Live Nation **Website:** www.ozzfest.com

Attendance at Oxegen is considered something of a rite of passage for Irish music-loving youngsters, such is its position as not only the biggest festival in Eire but also one of the largest in Europe. Oxegen has boasted gargantuan line-ups ever since its inception in 2004, with the premise being that if there isn't a musical act to your liking on offer then you really can't like music full stop. The energy and vibe is wild, the crowds even wilder; small wonder, then, that Oxegen landed the Best European Festival title at the public-voted Yourope Awards in 2008.

Oxegen's success is largely down to the promotional muscle provided by Denis Desmond's MCD Productions, one of the biggest festival promoters in the world. To say MCD have their fingers in a number of festival pies would be an understatement. MCD with Live Nation own a large share of Festival Republic (the organiser of the Reading, Leeds and Glastonbury festivals) while Desmond's Gaiety Investments has major stakes in the T In The Park, Isle of Wight and V festivals. The result is major clout in attracting the biggest names to its events.

Business aside, it's the sheer craic that makes Oxegen a must-visit on the festival calendar. The boys who love the black stuff have sure done well.

OXEGEN

Location: Punchestown Racecourse, County Kildare, Ireland **Founded:** 2004 **Current capacity:** 80,000 **Month:** July **Camping:** Yes (3 and 4 days) **Nearest airport:** Dublin **First headliners:** The Strokes, The Killers, The Cure, The Who, Basement Jaxx **Recent headliners:** Kings Of Leon, Rage Against The Machine, REM, The Verve **Promoter:** MCD Productions **Website:** www.oxegen.ie

JOHN PEEL PUKKELPOP PINKPOP

was lucky enough to share an office with John Peel for a number of years at BBC Radio 1. When I say 'share an office', don't imagine for an instant that it was just John and I lounging about in easy chairs playing records at the wrong speeds and swapping anecdotes about legendary Napalm Death gigs we'd attended. No. In my early days at Radio 1, it was John sitting in his usual spot surrounded by mountains of records, CDs, gold discs and teacups on one side of the office and me shyly skulking past to get to my desk, hoping he wouldn't notice me, such was my awe at being in the same room as the greatest broadcaster ever.

Later on, as our relationship blossomed, we regularly took the piss out of each other's oversized cagoules at various flooded festivals around the UK. John would chide both me and other Radio 1 staffers on why we hadn't marched halfway across the site to see some little-known wonder like Kanda Bongo Man (whom I later booked for Bestival on his advice) and chosen instead to see no-marks such as Primal Scream.

As everyone knows, John was an indefatigable festival goer who somehow popped up everywhere. He played records and introduced bands onstage at Reading Festival and Glastonbury (who later honoured him with the John Peel Stage for new bands), but it was his sets and words at Reading that created a new format for between-band-banter at festivals. He presented some incredibly entertaining Glasto television with Jo Whiley, often wearing ludicrous shorts in knee-deep mud while filling empty airtime when a band failed to take to the stage on time. And he DJed completely barmy sets at the Big Chill that joined the dots between happy hardcore and Status Quo. An absolute legend.

When festivals hit a certain size, they can often lose something of the vibe and spirit that made them so attractive in the first place. Not so Belgium's Pukkelpop. It may bring in more than 150,000 punters but it retains a quirky, individualistic air that continues to charm. It's the other 'stuff' that draws people back year after year. Recent highlights include singer Stijn Meuris giving an astronomical lecture; a Balkan circus tent; a 'cultural village' with bazaars and movies; a cinema tent screening nature documentaries and zombie flicks (perfect post-Metallica viewing); and free cycle racks to encourage visitors to get to the festival using pedal power. At the 2008 Yourope Awards Pukkelpop got the Green'n'Clean award too.

That said, as you'd expect with a festival of this calibre, musical line-ups are rock solid. The promoters seem to delight in mixing up acts with a reckless yet endearing sonic abandon; 2005 featured punk grungers the Pixies, legendary NYC outfit Dwarves, comedy rap merchants Goldie Lookin' Chain, weird electronicist Matthew Herbert and techno quarterback Darren Emerson. But the result is a festival that throws up surprises – musical and otherwise – which ain't bad considering that the organisers are led by a politician (Chokri Mahassine, who heads up the Humanistic Youth of Leopoldsburg).

PUKKELPOP

Location: Kempische Steenweg, Kiewit, Hasselt, Belgium **Founded:** 1985 **Current capacity:** 152,000 **Month:** August **Camping:** Yes

Nearest airport: Brussels **First headliners:** Front 242, Anne Clark, Anna Domino **Recent headliners:** Metallica, The Killers, Sigur Rós

Promoters: Humanistische Jongeren Leopoldsburg, Chokri Mahassine **Website:** www.pukkelpop.be

D on't be confused by the name; Gay Pride this ain't. The Netherlands' most famous outdoor festival is an unmissable fixture on every headbanger's calendar. It's been a metal and hard rock showcase for four decades with practically every star in the firmament shining here, including Metallica, ZZ Top, Iggy Pop And The Stooges, Van Halen and Rage Against The Machine. However, its legions of fans – more than 1.5 million tickets have been shifted to date – deserve more than a tarring of the monocultural rocker brush. The bill is tight, featuring just 40 acts over three days, but manages to shoe horn in a decent cross-section of musical genres, with Zero 7, The Specials, The Coral, Bentley Rhythm Ace, The Verve and Soulwax all treading the boards. There's also little to distract you from the proper business of festival going: this is not a land of hippy face-painting, just full-on moshing and drenching your fellow festival-goers in sweat. Weekend ticket-holders benefit from free camping too, with the sites offering civilised toilets, hot showers, supermarkets, cashpoints and food and drink.

If in doubt, pull out this trusty Dutch phrase at regular intervals – 'Ik hoor bij de band' ('I'm with the band') – or escape by hopping on the train to Amsterdam, found just 134 miles (two hours and 45 minutes) away to the north.

PINKPOP

Location: Landgraaf, Netherlands **Founded:** 1970 **Current capacity:** 60,000 **Month:** May/June **Camping:** Yes **Nearest airport:** Maastricht Aachen **First headliner:** Keef Hartley **Recent headliners:** Editors, Foo Fighters, Kaiser Chiefs, Queens Of The Stone Age **Promoters:** Buro Pinkpop BV and Mojo Concerts BV **Website:** www.pinkpop.nl

QUART QUEIMA DAS FITAS

The biggest of all the Norwegian music festivals, Quart is beloved of fans and musicians alike and has the knack of bringing out the best/worst in people. Maybe it's got something to do with the climate or the fact that it's located right in the middle of the Norwegian Bible Belt, but Quart has been the scene of some fairly outrageous behaviour over the years. A shotgun was fired from the stage in 1995; Marilyn Manson cancelled his 1999 show due to opposition from local religious groups; two members of rainforest charity group Fuck For Forest had sex on stage during a concert by The Cumshots; and black metallers Mayhem threw pig heads into the crowd in 2001. A family-friendly 'boutique festival' this is not.

The festival site itself is one of the most beautiful in northern Europe, a stunning park complete with pond for skinny dipping located just 20 yards from the main stage. Once the music stops at the main festival, many party heads relocate to the local town centre to hit up the bars and clubs as part of the more dance-orientated Klubb Quart events. The 2008 show was cancelled due to poor ticket sales but the 2009 event returned with former Guns N' Roses axesmith Slash rocking out in one of the headline slots.

QUART

Location: Kristiansand, Norway **Founded:** 1992 **Current capacity:** 40,000 **Month:** July **Camping:** Yes **Nearest airport:** Molde **First headliners:** Spiritualized, The Boo Radleys **Recent headliners:** The Who, Scissor Sisters, 50 Cent **Promoter:** Quartfestivalen **Website:** www.quart.no

As far as the festivals featured in this book go, the Queima das Fitas (Portuguese for 'Burning of the Ribbons') has one of the most interesting histories and most colourful climaxes. Organised by the University of Coimbra (the oldest in Portgugal), it's basically a week-long graduation bender for students, most of whom dress up in traditional gowns, top hats and walking sticks. Booze is everywhere – much of it free – and the aim for most is to slowly (or quickly) drink themselves into a stupor. Much of the action is centred around the city's old cathedral, with thousands attending a night-time *fado* serenade by students on the steps of the cathedral and in the square. Elsewhere, there are classical music recitals, discussions and lectures, and even karaoke.

The festival reaches a crescendo with the *cortejo* parade, which sees garishly decorated floats winding their way down from the hilltop university into the town centre. The event culminates with – yes, you guessed it – a big old ribbon-burning session, as graduates set fire to the colourful pieces of cloth that indicate which faculty they belong to. More than a few students end up in the river. Would you get away with this in the UK? No chance – Health & Safety wouldn't allow it. But here in laidback Portugal anything goes, even a little pyromania.

QUEIMA DAS FITAS

Location: University of Coimbra, Portugal **Founded:** Late nineteenth century **Current capacity:** Various **Month:** April/May **Camping:** No **Nearest airport:** Lisbon **First headliner:** None **Recent headliners:** None **Promoter:** University of Coimbra **Website:** www.queimadasfitas.org

READING FESTIVAL / LEEDS FESTIVAL **ROCKNESS** ROCK IN RIO
ROCK AM RING / ROCK IM PARK ROSKILDE BBC RADIO 1

READING

AUGUST BANK HOLIDAY WEEKEND

FRIDAY

rage against the machine

Queens of the Stone Age

THE FRATELLIS
THE ENEMY
The WOMBATS
VAMPIRE WEEKEND
MGMT

SATURDAY

THE KILLERS

BLOC PARTY
THE RACONTEURS
EDITORS
WE ARE SCIENTISTS
MANIC STREET PREACHERS
BULLET FROM MY VALENTINE
SEASICK STEVE

SUNDAY

METALLICA
Tenacious D
SLIPKNOT
FEEDER

THE CRIBS
THE LAST SHADOW PUPPETS
PENDULUM
CSS
SIMIAN MOBILE DISCO

READING FESTIVAL / LEEDS FESTIVAL

Location: Richfield Avenue, Reading, and Bramham Park, Leeds, UK **Founded:** 1971 **Current capacity:** 80,000 (Reading)/70,000 (Leeds)

Month: August **Camping:** Yes **Nearest airports:** Heathrow/Gatwick for Reading; Leeds for Bramham Park **First headliner:** Arthur Brown

Recent headliners: The Killers, Metallica **Promoter:** Festival Republic **Websites:** www.readingfestival.com/www.leedsfestival.com

O K, so you've done Glasto, but no hardcore festival-goer can hold their own around the camp fire without a stash of Reading anecdotes. This big beast started life as a jazz festival in Richmond in 1961, then went to dabble in punk and blues before metamorphosing into a lumbering rock and heavy metal monster, spitting out The Mission, Alice Cooper, Iggy Pop and The Sisters of Mercy into a sea of manic headbangers. These days, the three-dayer is one of the world's most successful festivals for a good reason: the formula has moved on beyond a spittle-soaked moshpit and massive beer tent. Underground and unsigned acts, punk, rap, hardcore and dance all get a look in and in 2008 attendees were also treated to a funfair, silent disco, air guitar contest, cinema and cabaret. And, just to prove how far the festival has come, there's now even a 'quieter' camping area and a clutch of 'podpads' and 'myhabs' (pre-erected mini-huts and tents to you and me) for the pickier camper.

But, although some acts may now be easier on the eardrums – with comparatively tuneful outfits such as British Sea Power and Arcade Fire treading the boards – the crowd has retained all of its legendary mercilessness, consistently dismissing below par performances with a shower of bottles and cans, some of them full of human waste! In 2008, enthusiastic Anglo-Saxon language and improvised missiles drove the FF'ers off stage – the kids

'The crowd has retained all of its legendary mercilessness, consistently dismissing below par performances with a shower of bottles and cans, some of them full of human waste!'

were disappointed to discover that they weren't the Foo Fighters after all – while rapper 50 Cent suffered a fierce hailstorm in 2004. Meat Loaf's 1988 exit remains one of the festival's finer putdowns: a flagon of cider (at least, we think it was cider) full in the face.

As you weave your way through the 191-acre site, you'll be stepping on hallowed musical ground too. Legendary janglers The Stone Roses indulged in their final spot of navel-gazing here in 1996, while Kevin Rowland of Dexy's Midnight Runners burst onto the stage flanked by strippers and wearing 'that dress' in 1999 – prompting a predictable response (see above). Top of the stunt charts has to be Kurt Cobain in 1992: Nirvana's lead singer rolled onto the stage in a wheelchair, a broken, hunched wreck of a man. It was OK though – it was just his dig at those speculating that he was a washed-up drug addict with months to live.

If you can't flog it to Reading, the festival's twin event in Leeds might fit the bill. Founded in 1999 to cater for increasing demand, the northern bash runs in parallel with its south-east sibling and features a near-identical line-up, just on different days.

Whichever you fancy, make sure you bag your tickets early. In 2008, all tickets to Reading/Leeds events sold out within 24 hours. And special mention to promoter Melvin Benn, one of the festival world's true pioneers.

Rockness has quickly established itself as a serious competitor in the Scottish market. How, you ask? Well, not only is it located on possibly the most beautiful festival site in the UK but whopping great acts such as The Prodigy, Manic Street Preachers, Biffy Clyro and Fatboy Slim literally queue up each year to ritually destroy the peace and quiet of the shores of Loch Ness. I've been to every one since it was founded in 2006 and – like fellow Scottish festival T In The Park – there's an insane atmosphere from the moment the gates open (or more accurately are thrown aside by the rabid party animals). Not until the last can of beer has been drunk and the sun rises on the Monday does the partying let up.

Personally, I get high from the invigorating fresh air (and a pint or four of Black Isle stout) and have had some of my most surreal festival experiences at Rockness, including talking to the eccentric guy who makes little Loch Ness monsters out of driftwood (and swears Nessie will surface at any minute) and holding onto the Inflatable Church by a guy-rope as it tried to fly off to Dundee on a particularly windy day. And it must be said: I've never had a better reception than in the Sunday Best DJ tent at Rockness faced by a sea of air horns, plus hands in the air and tops-off ravers chanting whatever it is they chant. Rock on!

ROCKNESS

Location: Dores, Scotland, UK **Founded:** 2006 **Current capacity:** 35,000 **Month:** June **Camping:** Yes **Nearest airport:** Inverness
First headliners: Fatboy Slim, Mylo, Carl Cox **Recent headliners:** Basement Jaxx, The Prodigy, Biffy Clyro **Promoter:** Loud Sound/AEG Live
Website: www.rockness.co.uk

ROCK IN RIO

Location: Lisbon and Arganda del Rey, Madrid **Founded:** 1985 **Current capacity:** 500,000 per festival **Month:** May and June (Lisbon), June and July (Madrid) **Camping:** Yes **Nearest airports:** Lisbon Portela, Madrid-Barajas **First headliner:** Queen **Recent headliners:** The Police, Lenny Kravitz, Metallica **Promoter:** Roberto Medina **Website:** www.rockinrio.com

More of a temporary metropolis than a rock festival, the first Rock in Rio treated 1.38 million punters to a bill of AC/DC, Ozzy Osbourne and Rod Stewart in a purpose-built 'city of rock'. Held over ten days in Rio de Janeiro, this vast celebration chimed with the optimism of the times, coinciding with the end of military rule. The monolith has now winged it across the Atlantic to Europe and although its capacity has been clipped en route, the bill retains its globe-straddling MOR ballast: Paul McCartney, Guns N' Roses and Britney Spears have put in appearances.

ROCK AM RING / ROCK IM PARK

Location: Nürburgring racetrack/Frankenstadion, Nürnberg, Germany **Founded:** 1985 **Current capacity:** 150,000 **Month:** June **Camping:** No **Nearest airports:** Cologne/Frankfurt **First headliners:** U2, Chris de Burgh, Joe Cocker **Recent headliners:** Rage Against The Machine, Metallica, The Prodigy **Promoter:** Marek Lieberberg **Website:** www.rock-am-ring.com

A double-header festival taking place in a racetrack and stadium in the west and south-east of Germany respectively. Although line-ups were somewhat middle of the road during the festival's early years (take a bow Huey Lewis and The News), these days you're likely to hear more contemporary acts such as Arctic Monkeys. Bands play both venues on consecutive days and the combined attendance makes it Germany's biggest music festival. Couple this with the Teutonic organisational ability and it is no surprise that tickets are like gold dust.

My first (and sadly only) trip to the ancient Viking city of Roskilde in the mid-90s was a real eye opener. Up until then I'd only witnessed UK shows with a diet of burger and chips swilled down with a trough of lager. Now here I was, snacking on sashimi and supping fine wines while watching Radiohead deliver their world-beating festi set. This was more like it! Started way back in 1971, Roskilde is one of Europe's four biggest shows and this is a festival with history – Bob Marley skanked onstage in 1978, U2 rocked it in '82 and Metallica, well, metalled in 1986. The 100,000 plus attendees are bolstered by 20,000 volunteers, making it a pleasant place to stay for the week of events.

Roskilde also has a very low crime rate, a solid green message and some innovative charity ideas involving mobile phones, beer cans and Africa in some way! It's also special in that most bands play in an array of tents ranging from tiny to vast, ensuring maximum intimacy and shelter from the unpredictable rain. Nearly all bands play proper concert-length hour-long shows too, unlike most other festies.

A terrible accident during Pearl Jam's performance in 2000 resulted in nine people dying, despite its record as probably the safest festival in Europe. The resulting tightening of safety measures even meant Glastonbury cancelled in 2001, to get itself up to Roskilde's level. Can I come back now, please?!

ROSKILDE

Location: Roskilde, Denmark **Founded:** 1971 **Current capacity:** 75,000 **Month:** July **Camping:** Yes **Nearest airport:** Copenhagen

First headliners: Tom Bailey, Alrune Rod, Spider John Koerner **Recent headliners:** The Chemical Brothers, Radiohead, Jay-Z

Promoter: Roskilde Festival **Website:** www.roskilde-festival.dk

K, so I'm biased but there's very little doubt that BBC Radio 1 is the finest radio station in the world. (Dispute that if you will, but I may politely ask you to step outside.) From Mary Anne Hobbs' championing of dubstep and Zane Lowe and Huw Stephen's breaking of new bands to Pete Tong's continued rule of all things dance and Chris Moyles' mammoth audience figures, Radio 1 is the place for new music in all its wondrous guises, from easy-on-the-ear pop to underground Egyptian gabba. That's radio-ga-ga alright.

So it comes as no surprise that Radio 1 has also championed and been at some of the best festivals around the UK and the wider world. I've DJed numerous times on the Radio 1 stage at Glastonbury, a glorious throbbing pyramid of sound and lights; Annie Nightingale's broadcasts from some sweaty breakbeat rave are the stuff of legend; and Jo Whiley and John Peel's epic Glastonbury TV and radio sessions are timeless. Who can forget when the Radio 1 generators all sunk under three feet of water and Whiley went off air or Peel having to fill time talking about what socks he was wearing as a band failed to take to the stage?

A stroke of genius was the set up of the BBC Introducing stage several years ago by live music boss Jason Carter, touring around festivals from Reading and Leeds to Latitude and Bestival, focusing on breaking new local acts wherever it landed. Radio 1's Big Day Out has been a massive success and individual festival efforts from Huw Stephens with his Swn festival in Cardiff and Gilles Peterson's Worldwide Festival in France to my own endeavours all continue to fly the Radio 1 flag. www.bbc.co.uk/radio1

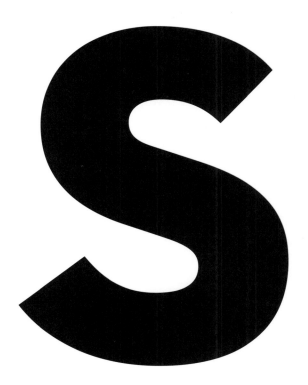

SÓNAR SNOWBOMBING STONEHENGE SECRET GARDEN PARTY
SUMMER SONIC SUMMERCASE SUNRISE CELEBRATION SPIRAL TRIBE
SHAMBALA REGGAE SUNSPLASH SZIGET

Situated smack in the middle of Barcelona and housed within an über-modern contemporary arts centre, museum and beautiful old church, Sónar has been sweating in the glorious Catalan sunshine for more than 16 years. It never fails to surprise and stimulate with a corking musical line-up alongside futuristic interactive art and technology shenanigans. Each year, around 80,000 open-minded and open-eared people from across the globe attend this 'annual festival of progressive music and multimedia arts', an event split into By Day and By Night – and I love it.

I've been a regular for the last six years – both as a DJ and as a hanger-around – and I always come away inspired, sunburned and half deaf. My average 'By Day' journey starts off with a lazy San Miguel-fuelled afternoon roasting in the sun, listening to abstract hip-hop, dubby techno and weird South American pop. During occasional trips into the pitch-dark installation spaces I've come across everything from a room full of nothing but bat-wing noises to a swing fitted with a video camera (that made me sick when I had a go).

After a quick change of shirt and dinner in one of Barcelona's amazing restaurants, it's off out of town to the cavernous warehouse spaces of 'By Night'. From the cream of adventurous electronic musicians (think Jeff Mills, Laurent Garnier, Yazoo, Pet Shop Boys, Björk) to the 'let's see who's got the daftest name' underground offerings from DJ Scotch Egg, Night Of The Brain and The Considerate Builders Scheme, Sónar is always *muy especial*.

SÓNAR

Location: Barcelona, Spain **Founded:** 1994 **Current capacity:** 80,000 **Month:** June **Camping:** No **Nearest airport:** Barcelona **First headliners:** Sven Väth, Laurent Garnier **Recent headliners:** Devo, Beastie Boys, Goldfrapp **Promoter:** Advanced Music S.L **Website:** www.sonar.es

O K, so let's cue the jokes about being 'on the piste'. Snowbombing is Europe's best winter sports and music festival. Currently held in the Austrian ski resort of Mayrhofen – after packed-out turns in France and Switzerland – it's also arguably Europe's most unique festival. Ski or board by day, rock out to big beats by night. It's an intoxicating combination, in more ways than one. DJs and dance music dominate the sonic menu (think Fatboy Slim, Mylo, Gilles Peterson) although more guitar-inclined acts such as Madness, The Pigeon Detectives and Dirty Pretty Things have made inroads of late. And while the quality of music on offer has undoubtedly been a major part in the ongoing success of the event – growing from a mere 250 souls in 2000 to more than 3,500 in 2008 – it's the location and atmosphere that are the real draw. Attendees can stay in a selection of civilised chalets and hotels while the bars and restaurants stay open real late to accommodate ravenous appetites. Meanwhile, parties and gigs happen in the most unusual locations, ranging from bird's nest-style huts to a nightclub in an igloo (yes, really).

Highlights of the week-long bash are legendary but the sight of hundreds of people skiing down the slopes in fancy dress, heading for the end-of-festival street party, is certainly one to behold. Some brave punters even do it naked. Yes, see you on the piste.

SNOWBOMBING

Location: Mayrhofen, Austria **Founded:** 2000 **Current capacity:** 3,500 **Month:** March/April **Camping:** No **Nearest airport:** Salzburg **First headliners:** Justin Robertson, Deadly Avenger, Aim **Recent headliners:** Fatboy Slim, Grandmaster Flash, Biffy Clyro **Promoter:** SBH Events **Website:** www.snowbombing.com

Stonehenge – the world-famous stone circle set in the heart of southern England – holds the honour of being the oldest 'festival' featured in this book, having hosted pagan rituals and druidic celebrations from when it was first erected circa 2,500BC. These days, access to the sacred circle is more controlled – there's a 50m exclusion zone around it in order to preserve the UNESCO World Heritage Site. But on the occasion of the summer solstice, the gates are thrown open to all and sundry and around 30,000 people descend on Stonehenge for a few hours of drumming, chanting, cosmic contemplation and spiritual enlightenment.

The solstice event attracts a ragtag bunch of traveller types, old-school ravers, sun worshippers and even bona fide druids, all there ready to go bananas when the sun rises around 5am. And although the British climate never guarantees a spectacular sun show, the result is always the same – lots of cheering, clapping and, er, 'freestyle' dancing. Whether you believe in all the attendant mystical mumbo jumbo or not, Stonehenge itself is a remarkable, dare we say it magical place, and the summer solstice a must-experience-at-least-once-in-your-lifetime event.

STONEHENGE

Location: Amesbury, Wiltshire, UK **Founded:** In the mists of time **Current capacity:** 30,000 **Month:** June **Camping:** No **Nearest airport:** Bristol **Website:** www.stonehenge.co.uk

Never before had I seen a wooden ship on a lake being shot at with burning arrows while a semi-naked Grace Jones sang *Pull Up To The Bumper* onstage and the girl in the lion outfit next to me somersaulted backwards, laughing and vomiting at the same time. Then again, I hadn't counted on the Secret Garden Party being quite as nuts as the first time I'd been, two years earlier. I parked my car in three feet of mud and allowed a small swamp to fill the footwell as I opened the door; I knew this would be fun. Set in a beautiful Cambridgeshire estate in the grounds of a Georgian farmhouse, the Secret Garden Party is consistently the most crazy and anarchic festival in the UK, but without the aggro or accidents. In its inaugural year, 2004, the stage manager was naked while the organiser – known as the Head Gardener – spent most of the weekend swimming around the lake. The next year the fancy dress theme was 'Dictators' and people threw themselves over giant pianos in the Suicide Olympics. When I last chipped up for a DJ set, I dropped acid-techno while sat in a treehouse overlooking a muddy field. It's all good.

A great British festival, then, and one that doesn't need big names or adverts to spoil the wicked word-of-mouth community it boasts. Secret – but not for long.

SECRET GARDEN PARTY

Location: Abbots Ripton, Huntingdon, Cambridgeshire, UK **Founded:** 2003 **Current capacity:** 10,000 **Month:** July **Camping:** Yes **Nearest airport:** Stansted **First headliners:** KT Tunstall, The Egg **Recent headliners:** Grace Jones, Florence and The Machine, Alphabeat **Promoter:** Secret Productions **Website:** www.secretgardenparty.com

SUMMER SONIC

Location: Osaka and Tokyo, Japan **Founded:** 2000 **Current capacity:** 200,000 **Month:** August **Camping:** Yes **Nearest airports:** Kansai International (Osaka), Narita (Tokyo) **First headliner:** John Spencer Blues Explosion **Recent headliners:** Coldplay, The Verve, Sex Pistols **Promoter:** Creativeman Productions **Website:** www.summersonic.com

With a grand finale firework display and oodles of top-quality sushi and teppan-yaki, this two-centre Japanese bash is hardly your standard festival. Add 100 acts, eight stages and home-grown talent such as chunky beat triumvirate Perfume and you have something remarkable on your hands. Summer Sonic spans three days and two locations, with bills bouncing between Osaka and Tokyo. The organisers are canny enough to bolster the native line-up with a raft of crowd pleasers too, so expect major international stars such as Coldplay and Alicia Keys.

SUMMERCASE

Location: Spain: Boadilla del Monte, Madrid; Parc del Fòrum, Barcelona **Founded:** 2006 **Current capacity:** 25,000 **Month:** July **Camping:** No **Nearest airports:** Madrid Barajas; El Prat, Barcelona **First headliner:** Daft Punk **Recent headliners:** Ian Brown, The Flaming Lips, Chemical Brothers **Promoter:** Sinnamon **Website:** www.summercase.com/indexen.html

Anybody who's necked a tequila or six in Spain will be aware of the natives' legendary appetite for all-night partying. No surprise, then, that the Summercase bash – held simultaneously in Barcelona and Madrid, with bands switching between cities – is a proper all-nighter, knocking off at 6am. Each event boasts five stages and a bill that bucks the Iberian obsession with strutting rock; Foals, Lily Allen and Interpol mixing it with resuscitated legends such as the Happy Mondays. Go for the Barcelona bash and you can sleep it off on the beach.

SUNRISE CELEBRATION

Location: Yeovil, Somerset, UK **Founded:** 2006 **Current capacity:** 5,000 **Month:** May/June **Camping:** Yes **Nearest airports:** Bristol/Exeter

First headliner: Dreadzone **Recent headliners:** The Orb, System 7 **Promoter:** Natural Communities CIC **Website:** www.sunrisecelebration.com

Like a Glasto without the brain-numbing crowds or prize arses, Sunrise Celebration puts the welly wanging back into the UK festival scene. Founded to coincide with the UK's summer solstice, the festival lays down a hatful of dub, ska, electronica, reggae, Balkan beats and more on a breezy organic Somerset farm. It's 100 per cent green-powered, with friendly eco-rangers on hand 24 hours a day. Breaks between dream healing workshops can be filled by a wander through the site: the place is awash with minstrels, stilt-walkers, astrologers, breakdancers and the odd spot of duelling. There's bags to entertain the kids too, including a disco, circus and bushcraft sessions.

SPIRAL TRIBE

Location: Various global locations **Founded:** 1990 **Current capacity:** Various **Month:** Throughout the year **Camping:** Yes **Nearest airports:** Various **First headliners:** None **Recent headliners:** None **Promoter:** Spiral Tribe **Website:** www.spiral-tribe.org

The Spiral Tribe free party collective sprang up from the acid house and traveller communities and was responsible for a string of illegal raves and festivals throughout the UK in the early 90s. Their high watermark of fame came in 1992 when they acted as the catalyst for the Castlemorton Common Festival, a week-long bender that attracted 40,000 people and a host of tabloid headlines and resulted in crushing new anti-liberty laws from the government. Following a high-profile court case against the group (that collapsed at a cost to the taxpayer of £4m), the collective later dispersed to the US and Europe. Spiral Tribe resurfaced in 2007, issuing new music via their website.

Like some sort of old-school rave, Shambala's organisers reveal neither the festival's location nor its performers in advance. You get the venue details upon ticket purchase and you'll find out who's playing when you get there. It's a pot-luck approach but one that's successfully come up trumps year after year. The festival itself actually has rave-like beginnings, starting out as a party for 150 souls in a field with a borrowed sound system and a stage mounted on a friendly farmer's trailer. With zero advertising (and no sponsorship), Shambala has since grown purely through word of mouth and these days is a family-friendly affair with an emphasis on creativity, green issues and surprise entertainment. Yes, there's a dance tent and even a main stage but there's also much good old-fashioned British eccentricity, with past highlights including a massive fancy dress party, a speakers' corner, giant inflatables for the kids, a Geisha makeover service and even a bedtime story tent.

Above all, it's all about participating in rather than just watching the action. Enrol in a samba lesson, jig along at a barn dance, make jewellery in the craft area or get up on stage to exorcise those poetry demons – Shambala has done much to unleash the inner creative and is one of the most original of the UK's boutique festivals.

SHAMBALA

Location: Secret stately home grounds in Northamptonshire **Founded:** 1999 **Current capacity:** 7,000 **Month:** August **Camping:** Yes

Nearest airports: Various **Recent headliners:** The Beat, The Nextmen, Kid Kanevil **Promoter:** Shambala **Website:** www.shambalafestival.org

t helped propel Bob Marley to global superstardom, taught white men to dance during tours of North America and Europe and has finally come home to its roots. Reggae Sunsplash was first staged by Synergy Productions in Jamaica in 1978 and lit the touchpaper for Jamaica's festival scene, going on to showcase some of reggae's biggest stars over the next 21 years including Gregory Isaacs, Stevie Wonder, Peter Tosh and Steel Pulse. The death of some of the festival's founders led to a hiatus, but it was relaunched by Kenny Benjamin in Jamaica in 2006, unleashing a new crop of acts including Beenie Man and Vybz Kartel. Today's festival couldn't have found a better home: it's held on a 200-acre site in Marley's birthplace parish of St Ann, flanked by the towering Blue Mountains and the Caribbean Sea. The 'roots, rock and reggae' formula offers more than 100 acts over four nights, with themed sessions covering genres such as dancehall and world beat. And beyond the two main stages you'll find dance and poetry (Steppa, Dingo and Payne have all read here) alongside family activities, arts and crafts, a huge food court and that staple of Jamaican celebrations, a dominoes play area.

Ever suffering from itchy feet, Reggae Sunsplash is touring again, with dates scheduled for Brazil and Florida.

REGGAE SUNSPLASH

Location: Priory, St Ann, Jamaica **Founded:** 1978 **Current capacity:** 150,000 **Month:** August **Camping:** Yes **Nearest airport:** Montego Bay, Jamaica **First headliners:** Peter Tosh, Bob Marley & The Wailers, Dennis Brown **Recent headliners:** Luciano, UB40, Marley, Toots and The Maytals **Promoter:** Reggae Sunsplash International **Website:** www.reggaesunsplashja.com

s greedy moneymen turn so many festivals into clone cash machines, central Europe's largest gig – with 1,000-plus artists and 60-plus venues – swims heroically against the tide. Founded to fill a gap after the fall of Communism, Sziget occupies a utopian setting: more than 100 acres of traffic-free, tree-clad island on the Danube between Buda and Pest. And while the bill is important – featuring usual festival-slayers such as the Sex Pistols and the Kaiser Chiefs – it's the stuff seeping into the cracks that gives the event its cachet. Campers have a tendency to pitch up wherever they fancy, giving the week-long bash an organic vibe. There are excellent food and booze options together with an entire village-worth of activities and events, from salsa classes and a circus to cinema, ballet, theatre, bungee jumping, volleyball and a footie pitch.

For those interested in checking out the tunes, Euro rock and metal dominate (Iron Maiden, Hungary's Al-Om) with occasional forays into stomp-along favourites from bands such as Flogging Molly and The Cribs. Beyond the main stages, though, there's a good choice of jazz, world, electronica, classical and dance, with Hungarian ska-meisters Pannonia Allstars Ska Orchestra and Róisín Murphy laying on some of the finest sets in 2008.

In true egalitarian style, festival organisers also operate a 'wish list' to elicit ideas for forthcoming line-ups.

SZIGET

Location: Óbudai-sziget, Budapest, Hungary **Founded:** 1993 **Current capacity:** 400,000 **Month:** August **Camping:** Yes **Nearest airport:** Budapest Ferihegy **First headliner:** Hobo Blues Band **Recent headliners:** Iron Maiden, REM, Lauren Harris **Promoter:** Sziget Kulturális Szervezőiroda **Website:** www.sziget.hu/festival_english

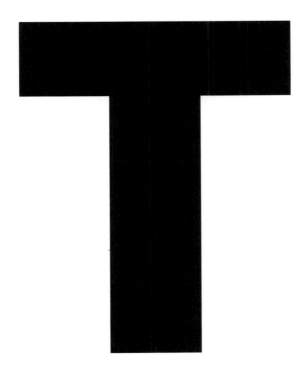

SUNDAY best

WEIRD WEST

T IN THE PARK FESTIVAL TRANS MUSICALES DE RENNES
TRUCK TRIBAL GATHERING TDK TIME WARP

Scotland's biggest festival puts hot cake vending in the proverbial shade: tickets are practically jet-propelled, the entire stash selling out in around two hours flat in 2008. The reason is simple: I occasionally DJ there. Oh ok so it's not a Rob da Bank techno set that gets half of Scotland down to Kinross but the grade-A festi line-up. A kind of concentrated Glastonbury, it manages to attract both bands at the top of their game (think Kaiser Chiefs and the Fratellis) and perennial legends (The Pogues being prime examples) while dipping a toe into the zeitgeist with names such as Bombay Bicycle Club and Mr Hudson & The Library. And although established rock and indie acts are the heroes, T Break and Futures stages showcase unsung talent, and the 12,000-capacity Slam Tent lays on the big beats from the likes of Josh Wink, Aphex Twin and Erol Alkan. Even the fervent nationalist gets a good return on the ticket price: Ian Brown brought on the bagpipes in 2008 while Biffy Clyro and Paolo Nutini have also whipped crowds into a frenzy.

The event salves your conscience too: it became the world's biggest carbon-neutral festival in 2006 and is steaming ahead with initiatives such as deposits on beer cups (yes, people actually bring them back), offsetting emissions by funding forestry projects and recycling. Be sure to buy your tickets from the official site (see below) and not the many unauthorised websites.

T IN THE PARK

Location: Balado, Kinross-shire, Scotland **Founded:** 1994 **Current capacity:** 85,000 **Month:** July **Camping:** Yes **Nearest airport:** Glasgow
First headliner: Moby **Recent headliners:** The Verve, REM, The Chemical Brothers **Promoter:** DF Concerts **Website:** www.tinthepark.com

The Festival Trans Musicales de Rennes (Transmusicales for short) is a three-day celebration of new music held in Rennes, Brittany, and is considered one of the granddaddies of the festival circuit. It started in 1979 with a bold mission statement – 'What we are about, what we want to do is defend and promote a new vision of music that differs from what the public is being force-fed' – and has maintained a progressive stance ever since. Transmusicales is one of those places where they are completely justified in saying 'You heard it here first'.

Thanks in part to its winter timing and a giant shed location close to Rennes airport, Transmusicales is a favourite quick visit for music biz types who like to jet in to catch the hottest new bands. Although there are no official headliners, artists of the calibre of the Beastie Boys, Coldcut, Primal Scream and Clap Your Hands Say Yeah have graced the festival at some point while both Björk and Nirvana made their French debuts there. Scheduling is similarly eclectic; 1999 saw gangster rap innovators Public Enemy preceded onstage by the Qawwali Brothers, exponents of Sufi devotional music.

Festival director Jean-Louis Brossard has been in the hot seat since the event's inception but shows no sign of resting on his laurels; in 2006 Transmusicales decamped to Beijing, China, for a special three-day edition, following previous one-dayers in Switzerland and Norway.

FESTIVAL TRANS MUSICALES DE RENNES

Location: Parc Expo de Rennes, Brittany, France **Founded:** 1979 **Current capacity:** 23,000 **Month:** December **Camping:** No **Nearest airport:** Rennes **First headliners:** Marquis de Sade **Recent headliners:** Esser **Promoter:** Loi de 1901 Terrapin **Website:** www.lestrans.com

As free-range shindigs go, this festival is clucking first class. Robin Bennett founded Truck as an antidote to sprawling, corporate-riddled behemoths, rustling up a few flat-bed trucks to build a makeshift stage on an Oxfordshire farm. More than a decade on, the 'gig in a barn meets village fête' ethic is pretty much intact: nosh is provided by the Rotary Club and served by farmers, a vicar peddles ice lollies, a dedicated bus minimises emissions and a gaggle of stalls sell crafts and clothes. Even PR campaigns have a folksy charm: the 2008 festival was launched at a city farm in London.

Organisers like to keep their powder dry on line-up announcements, but expect six stages featuring cult act such as Noah And The Whale, a sprinkling of legends – Small Faces' Ian McLagan and The Lemonheads have performed – and some genuine stonkers such as Get Cape, Wear Cape, Fly.

And if 5,000 people sounds like a bit of crush, head for Truck's sister festival, Wood, held in May in a nearby eco-village. Limited to just 1,000 people, this family-orientated event features coppicing workshops, yurts and old-skool sing-alongs around the campfire. Even its two stages, hosting mainly acoustic acts, boast impeccable green credentials – one is powered by the sun, the other by a bicycle.

TRUCK

Location: Hill Farm, Steventon, Oxfordshire, UK **Founded:** 1998 **Current capacity:** 5,000 **Month:** July **Camping:** Yes
Nearest airport: Heathrow **First headliner:** Wonderland **Recent headliners:** The Lemonheads, Idlewild, The Futureheads
Promoter: Truck **Website:** www.thisistruck.com

TRIBAL GATHERING

Location: Lower Pertwood Farm, Wiltshire, UK/Luton Hoo, Bedforshire, UK **Founded:** 1993 **Capacity:** 30,000 **Camping:** No **Nearest airports:** N/A **First headliners:** Laurent Garnier, Carl Cox, Paul Oakenfold **Recent headliners:** Kraftwerk, Orbital, Laurent Garnier **Promoter:** Universe

What Woodstock was to hippies, Tribal Gathering was for ravers. Following the spirit of illegal outdoor raves such as Sunrise and Raindance, Tribal Gathering was the ultimate melting pot of hippies, crusties, trustafarians, city boys and semi-naked people, all trance-dancing with eyes closed and arms aloft. The precursor to big dance festivals Creamfields and Global Gathering, Tribal only had one year as a truly underground happening before the UK's draconian Criminal Justice Act unplugged our speakers and confiscated our headphones. It was probably a good thing for Tribal though, as it then teamed up with the Mean Fiddler to present The Prodigy (1995) and Kraftwerk (1997). It all wrapped up a year later but while it may be gone it's certainly not forgotten.

TDK TIME WARP

Location: Mannheim, Germany **Founded:** 1994 **Month:** April **Camping:** No **Nearest airports:** Frankfurt/Stuttgart **First headliners:** Speedy J, John Acquaviva **Recent headliners:** Ricardo Villalobos, Carl Cox, Laurent Garnier **Promoter:** Cosmopop **Website:** www.time-warp.de

With stellar line-ups featuring the likes of Sven Väth, Richie Hawtin and Ricardo Villalobos, you'd be forgiven for thinking that Time Warp was just one big minimal techno love-in. In actual fact the eight-day festival takes over the southern German town of Mannheim and fills every nook and cranny with a huge variety of 'electronic lifestyle' gatherings, proving that Time Warp is about more than just the music. In addition to the broad range of club and gig events are the 'Lab' series of workshops and seminars and a 'Media & Arts' strand.

UNDERAGE UKULELES UMBRIA JAZZ FESTIVAL ULTRA MUSIC FESTIVAL

For once, 'getting down with the kids' rings true. Billed as the 'world's first strictly 14 to under 19s credible music festival' (no one over the wrinkly old age of 18 can buy a ticket), this teenage festival lugs a heavily doodled knapsack of rock, indie and electronica to London's Victoria Park. Although it sounds like a harebrained splicing of *St Trinian's* and *Buffy the Vampire Slayer*, the shindig is far more than a load of floppy-fringed McFly wannabes cotching down sans mouldies. The one-dayer marshals five stages sponsored by credible brands such as NME, Converse and Topman, while there's a decent jam section and DJ tent hosting spinmeisters such as Good Shoes, Kid Harpoon and Young Turks. The bill isn't overrun with teeny-bopper lightweights either: acts have included hip-hop star Dizzee Rascal, indie popsters Mumm-Ra (voted as one of NME's best new bands) and Charlatans frontman Tim Burgess on the decks.

There are some clever table-turning touches too. Adults are dropped off in a crèche for collection at close of play, and the toe-curling interminable jams of yesteryear are banned, with sets limited to a neat 20-30 minutes. Bar the fact that kick-out time is 8pm and there are zero drugs and alcohol, the event feels like a bona fide festival – albeit in an oldie-free fantasy land.

UNDERAGE

Location: Victoria Park, London, UK **Founded:** 2007 **Current capacity:** 7,500 **Month:** August **Camping:** No **Nearest airports:** London City/ Heathrow **First headliner:** Patrick Wolf **Recent headliners:** Bombay Bicycle Club, Foals, Gallows **Promoters:** Underage Club and Eat Your Own Ears **Website:** www.underagefestivals.com

**W**hat is it about a ukulele that seems to strike a chord, pardon the pun, with festival crowds? Maybe it's because you can wave it around while pretending to be Slash/Noel Gallagher/that guy with the long fringe out of Bloc Party who is bloody good on the guitar. Or perhaps it's because it's one of the only musical instruments that not only fits in your rucksack but also acts as a suitably hefty deterrent to smash any would-be tent thief around the head as he tries to nab that 367,000MB iPod that you so wisely brought to a show where the music never stops. Either way, they've now become one of the must-have accessories on the boutique festival circuit; you simply can't be seen in your limited-edition Maharishi moleksin shorts and Jimmy Choo wellies at Bestival/The Big Chill/Secret Garden Party without a customised ukulele strung across your back.

When I invited the Dulwich Ukulele Orchestra to bring their Night Of 100 Ukes session to the main stage at Bestival, I'd never seen such a frightened stage manager. There he was, poor bloke, faced with 100 sunburnt and pissed uke players stumbling onstage to a huge roar from the crowd as they embarked upon a ramshackle rendition of Johnny Cash's 'Ring Of Fire'. Ukeing brilliant.

ny jazzman worth his salt – from the mighty Miles Davis to good-time swingster Ray Gelato – has blown his horn at this daddy of a festival, held in the heart of Italy. Billed as one of Europe's best jazz bashes, it's now a two-headed beast with a summer event in Perugia and a winter noodle-athon in Orvieto. Both the Italian towns are high-altitude gems – Orvieto sits on a huge plinth of volcanic rock – which only helps to heighten the heady mix of quality tunes, medieval squares and rammed streets.

In Perugia, you're as far from Glasto mud and soggy rizlas as you can get. The entire Centro Storico is turned over to the event, with more than 500 musicians playing 250 sessions in theatres, open-air stages and on the Duomo's sweeping steps. There's a steady stream of alcohol – mini bars line the main drag of Corso Vannucci – but remarkably few high jinks. The open access formula also means that even the terminally disorganised can enjoy the vibe without booking months in advance. That said, it's worth bagging tickets for a few prime sets before you arrive if you can, particularly if you want to catch bigger cheeses such as Gilberto Gil or Paolo Conte.

Orvieto is a more intimate affair, with performances by acts such as the Joe Locke Quartet and the Harlem Jubilee Singers taking place in Teatro Mancinelli and historical palazzi throughout town.

UMBRIA JAZZ FESTIVAL

Location: Perugia and Orvieto, Umbria, Italy **Founded:** 1973 **Current capacity:** Varies **Month:** July (Perugia), December/January (Orvieto) **Camping:** No **Nearest airports:** Perugia/Rome **First headliners:** Mal Waldron, Weather Report, Sun Ra **Recent headliners:** REM, Herbie Hancock, Sonny Rollins, BB King **Promoter:** European Jazz Festivals Organization **Website:** www.umbriajazz.com

Let's not beat about the bush: the two-day Ultra Music Festival is America's biggest and most important dance music bash. Taking place in the middle of the Winter Music Conference – a week-long industry backslapathon featuring everyone who's anyone in the dance music business – UMF brings the genre's biggest hitters to the masses. DJs and producers alike plan their annual calendars around the festival, ensuring that they have the freshest, newest music to launch at the event. Climate, timing and location undoubtedly play a big part in UMF's success. Miami in late March is a more than agreeable place to be – not only is it the WMC but it's also spring break (the annual easter holiday for US college students) and there's something rather special about playing on a beach in broad daylight to an audience that seems to comprise mainly buffed-up men and bikini-clad girls. But getting back to the music, it's the sheer strength of the line-ups that attract the crowds. Interestingly, UMF is also the place where more indie-inclined bands attempt to hit up the electronica-loving audiences: The Cure, The Killers and Bloc Party have all performed at the event.

The UMF brand has recently exported further afield, hosting events in Sao Paulo, Belo Horizonte, San Juan, Madrid and Ibiza.

ULTRA MUSIC FESTIVAL

Location: Bicentennial Park, Miami, USA **Founded:** 1999 **Current capacity:** 55,000 **Month:** March **Camping:** No **Nearest airport:** Miami
First headliners: Paul van Dyk, Rabbit In The Moon, LTJ Bukem **Recent headliners:** The Prodigy, Paul van Dyk, Tiësto, Bloc Party **Promoter:** Ultra Music Festival Productions **Website:** www.ultramusicfestival.com

V FESTIVAL VOODOO EXPERIENCE **RHYTHM AND VINES VIRTUAL FESTIVALS**

One day in 1995, Pulp frontman Jarvis Cocker had a dream. Wouldn't it be great, he mused, to play two massive open-air gigs over successive days. Richard Branson's Virgin empire granted the elbow patch-sporting bespectacled Yorkshireman his wish, bolted on a few indie stablemates and, in 1996, the V Festival was born. The event now sports one of the biggest pairs of wellies – alongside T in the Park, Reading, Leeds and Glastonbury – in the UK festival field. The trailblazing two-centre format – where bands play two sites on alternate days – has been much imitated and the V brand has since spread to the US, Canada and Australia. It is one of the most succesful festival brands worldwide.

Yes some naysayers criticise the festi for being one big, slick, MOR, travelling billboard for the Virgin brand. (Branson, a clever self-publicist? Surely not.) But while many areas are logo-emblazoned, you can't deny the massive line-up and annual sell out of tickets.

V FESTIVAL

Location: Hylands Park, Chelmsford and Weston Park, Staffordshire, UK; US; Canada; Australia **Founded:** 1996 **Current capacity:** Hylands Park and Weston Park, 90,000 **Month:** UK, August; Australia, March and April; US, August; Canada, June **Camping:** Yes **Nearest airports:** Chelmsford, Stansted; Weston Park, Birmingham International **First headliner:** Pulp **Recent headliners:** Muse, The Verve, Radiohead, Morrissey **Promoters:** Virgin Media/SJM/Metropolis, UK; IMP Productions, USA **Website:** music.virgin.com/festivals

VOODOO EXPERIENCE

Location: New Orleans City Park, Louisiana, USA **Founded:** 1999 **Current capacity:** 150,000 **Month:** October **Camping:** No **Nearest airport:** Louis Armstrong International **First headliners:** Moby, Wyclef Jean **Recent headliners:** Smashing Pumpkins, Red Hot Chili Peppers, REM **Promoter:** Rehage Entertainment **Website:** www.thevoodooexperience.com

You can't keep a good festival down. Hurricane Katrina may have all but wiped New Orleans off the map in 2005, but Voodoo Experience organisers pressed ahead in any case, holding a free event just two months later for all those lending a hand in the rescue and clean-up operation. The festival, held in a pastoral setting among lagoons and oak trees, retains all of its defiance, serving up three days of guitar-based thrashing (Stone Temple Pilots, Nine Inch Nails), rock musing (REM), sing-along angst-ridden pop (Panic at the Disco), soul, rap and R'n'B.

RHYTHM AND VINES

Location: Waiohika Estate, Gisborne, New Zealand **Founded:** 2003 **Current capacity:** 20,000 **Month:** December/January **Camping:** Yes **Nearest airport:** Gisborne **First headliner:** The Black Seeds **Recent headliners:** Franz Ferdinand, The Kooks, Santogold **Promoters:** Paxton Talbot, Hamish Pinkham, Toby Burrows and Scott Witters **Website:** www.rhythmandvines.co.nz

Rhythm and Vines is the only festival in this book to be staged over New Year's Eve – New Zealand is thankfully in the middle of summer right then. But hearing 20,000 festival nutters scream 'Happy New Year!' is not its only selling point – there's the awesome scenic location (a working vineyard), quality bands, jaw-dropping firework display, 25m waterslide and infamous Kiwi hospitality. The partying rarely stops at midnight, with most revellers staying up to welcome the first sunrise of the year around 6am – so be prepared to party long and hard.

uch like Heat magazine if you want to know what Cheryl Cole had for breakfast, or Radio 4 if you're after the ins and outs of fiscal policy in Tanzania, Virtual Festivals is the oracle of all things festivals. Having started a decade ago VF (as those in the know call them) are more than equipped to call themselves 'the number one source of festival info', although competitor eFestivals may debate that. Personally, I graze gossip and information off both sites most weeks, but what I like about VF is keeping up to speed on the latest gossip with their desktop alerts. Their homepage is clear and concise, there are cracking interviews, great photo and video libraries and, perhaps most importantly, they're stretching the boundaries and moving out of the UK into Europe and beyond. In fact VF are on the verge of launching a European portal and with such a wealth of amazing festivals across the Channel this can only be a good thing (so long as everyone doesn't go abroad for their festival fix!).

Last but not least, the boys had the rather good idea of launching their own awards show a few years back which has gone from a mildly shambolic affair to the place to be seen suited and booted as you pick up the gong for Best New Festival, Best Toilet Roll Used or Best Festival For Old Aged Pensioners. **www.virtualfestivals.com**

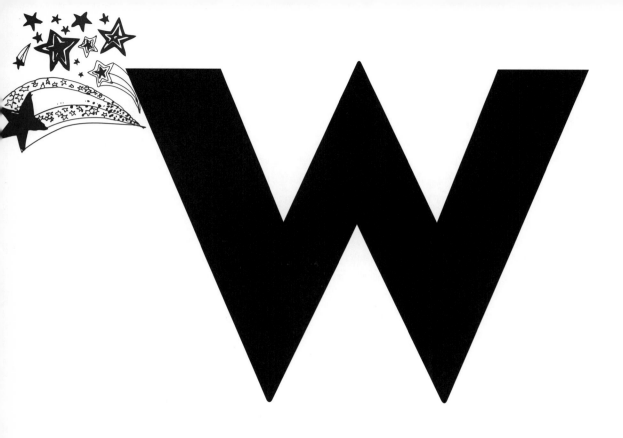

WOODSTOCK THE WICKERMAN FESTIVAL WOMAD

WOODSTOCK

Location: Bethel, New York, USA **Founded:** 1969 **Capacity:** 500,000 **Month:** August **Camping:** Yes **Nearest airport:** JFK, New York **First headliners:** Joan Baez, The Grateful Dead, The Who, Jimi Hendrix **Promoter:** Woodstock Ventures **Website:** www.woodstockmuseum.org

Peace, love and Jimi Hendrix deconstructing 'The Star Spangled Banner'. The 1969 Woodstock festival represented the high watermark of the hippie movement, a glorious sun-beaten love-in of good vibes, outstanding musical performances and screw-The-Man attitude. It all began when financiers John Roberts and Joel Rosenman placed an advertisement in the *New York Times* looking for business opportunities. Promoters Michael Lang and Artie Kornfeld responded and between them they came up with the idea for Woodstock, eventually staging it on land owned by Elliot Tiber and Max Yasgur. Some 186,000 tickets were sold prior to the concert but when more than 500,000 people showed up the fences were torn down and entry was made free. Financially speaking, the festival lost a packet.

Many of the big acts of the day performed at Woodstock – The Who, Crosby Stills Nash & Young, Jefferson Airplane, Creedence Clearwater Revival, Janis Joplin, Joan Baez – although Tiber summed it up best: 'For Kornfeld, Woodstock wasn't a matter of building stages, signing acts or even selling tickets. For him, the festival was always a state of mind, a happening that would exemplify the generation.'

Michael Wadleigh's documentary of the event is rightly celebrated. Not only did it capture the genesis and flowering of a one-of-a-kind happening – warts and all – it was innovative in its use of multiple camera angles and soundtracks. Compiled from more than 120 miles of film footage, it deservedly bagged the Best Documentary

gong at the 1971 Oscars, even if it didn't feature The Grateful Dead (who requested their performance be omitted from the movie). In 2008 the Bethel Woods Center for the Arts opened on the original site to commemorate the festival and its legacy. Just don't touch the brown acid!

Footnote: If Woodstock 1969 is regarded as a shining light of music festival culture, the revival 30 years later was, by most yardsticks, an unmitigated disaster. Fuelled by searing heat, inadequate sanitation and eye-popping prices for food and water, the event descended into a miasma of pyromania, looting, rioting and worse. Things got so hairy that MTV pulled out its entire film crew, with host Kurt Loder describing the scene as 'like a concentration camp'. Meanwhile Red Hot Chili Peppers frontman Anthony Kiedis likened the view from the stage to the Vietnam film *Apocalypse Now*. After the event, police opened investigations into four alleged rapes.

ORIGINAL WOODSTOCK PROMOTER MICHAEL LANG SPEAKS

Did you ever envisage that Woodstock would become the festival that everyone still talks about? Certainly not beforehand but once we were into it it was obvious this was something unique in our history. **Who was your favourite act?** Sly And The Family Stone took us all higher. **How do you explain the masses that turned up?** We planned on 200,000 and knew about a week before when we had sold 150,000 in advance that we were in for some sort of record numbers. We were lucky that the estimated million on the roads never managed to get there. **Do you wish Woodstock was still going today?** You can never step in the same river twice but the spirit still lives on. Obama's election was certainly a Woodstock moment. **What was the best thing about Woodstock?** The people. **What was the scariest thing about Woodstock?** The people! **What music are you listening to today?** My Morning Jacket and Coldplay. **What festivals do you admire?** New Orleans Jazz & Heritage, Coachella, Bonnaroo and Glastonbury all have unique characters.

lthough filmed on a shoestring budget and featuring little in the way of blood and gore, *The Wicker Man* is regarded as one of the finest British horror films ever made. Starring Christopher Lee, it centres on the pagan rituals of an isolated island community and culminates in a terrifying final scene where a policeman (played by Edward Woodward) is burned to death inside a 40-foot-high human effigy made of – you guessed it – wicker. The film is also the inspiration for this small but perfectly formed family-friendly festival that takes place in the area of the Scottish Highlands where the movie was shot. Ritual human sacrifice is not part of today's festival but a wickerman is still ceremoniously torched on the Saturday night.

As befitting an event that landed a Best Grass Roots Festival gong at the 2007 UK Festival Awards, Wickerman eschews crass commercialisation, lager sponsorship and other enormo-festival trappings for a more DIY, craft-based approach. Music-wise it's widescreen, with tents and stages devoted to acoustic performance, reggae and world music alongside the headlining acts. Tepees and yurts are available if you don't fancy camping in a tent and there are bags of activities to entertain the little 'uns. Short of Britt Ekland repeating her naked dancing from the film, we can't think of anything that would make this festival better than it already is.

THE WICKERMAN FESTIVAL

Location: East Kirkcarswell Farm, near Dundrennan, Scotland, UK **Founded:** 2002 **Current capacity:** 15,000 **Month:** July **Camping:** Yes **Nearest airport:** Edinburgh **First headliners:** Spear of Destiny, Stiff Little Fingers, UK Subs **Recent headliners:** KT Tunstall, Gary Numan, Alabama 3 **Promoter:** The Wickerman Festival Ltd **Website:** www.thewickermanfestival.co.uk

Peter Gabriel has a lot to answer for. Back in his hirsute heyday, the prog rocker decided western ears needed respite from the chart-topping pop of Duran Duran and Spandau Ballet and pieced together an eclectic bill of gospel, Latin, folk, rock, reggae, jazz and dance. More than 25 years on, the World Of Music, Arts And Dance is a global franchise, spreading its tie-dyed tendrils across Europe, New Zealand, Australia, Japan, Denmark, Canada, the US and, in 2009, the Middle East. The daddy, however, remains the UK event, transplanted to the sunny uplands of Wiltshire in 2007 after a 20-year residency in Reading. More than 70 bands descend on a country estate, joined by DJs, workshops and cookery classes, installation art and a vast 'global village' bristling with cuisine and crafts.

The line-up remains as 'worldy' as ever with regular blasts of the Moroccan sintir (lute) and the Chinese sheng (reed pipe), and bands hailing from more than 40 countries: Mongolia's Altai Kai, Egypt's Bedouin Jerry Can Band and Japan's taiko drummers Gocoo have all appeared. Happily, those bobbing in a sea of confusion can cling to big name life rafts such as Eddy Grant and The Frontline Orchestra, Ernest Ranglin, Lee 'Scratch' Perry and Nitin Sawhney. And despite recent luxury twiddles such as pre-erected tepees and a spa, the laid-back, kid-friendly, kaftan and joss stick formula endures.

WOMAD

Location: Charlton Park, Malmesbury, Wiltshire, UK; New Zealand; Australia; Spain; Gran Canaria **Founded:** 1982 **Current capacity:** 25,000 (UK) **Month:** July (UK) **Camping:** Yes (UK only) **Nearest airport:** Bristol (UK) **First headliner:** Echo & The Bunnymen **Recent headliners:** Seun Kuti, Rachid Taha, Speed Caravan, Martha Wainwright **Promoter:** Womad Ltd **Website:** www.womad.org

SXSW – SOUTH BY SOUTHWEST

As important as the Miami Winter Music Conference is for dance heads, South By Southwest (SXSW) is the most impactful event in the global music industry calendar for anyone into new indie bands and rock acts. Each year, more than 12,000 delegates (and thousands more punters) descend on Austin, Texas, to meet, greet and check out hot new bands and DJs. Deals are struck, friendships forged and careers kick-started; The Darkness got their first breaks at SXSW while the likes of Franz Ferdinand, The Kooks and the Kaiser Chiefs also upped their standing there.

Not only is SXSW an essential pit stop to make it in the biz, it's also a $110 million boost to the local economy. The sheer volume and choice of acts on show is breathtaking, with more than 1,400 performances crammed into dozens of Austin venues during the central four-day session. And the workshops, panel discussions and networking sessions are hugely popular too; David Byrne from Talking Heads and Pete Townshend from The Who were among those who spoke in '07. For the last two years, I have hosted Rob da Bank & Friends events, too.

Never one to rest on their laurels, the SXSW team tapped into Austin's burgeoning reputation as a cultural hotbed by adding film and interactive conferences to the main music happenings, expanding the whole event to a Texas-sized ten-day session. And they are partners in the three-day North By Northeast (NXNE) festival in Toronto, Canada, which takes place every June. Oh yeah and the tequila's pretty fierce too!

SXSW – SOUTH BY SOUTHWEST

Location: Austin Convention Center, Austin, Texas, USA **Founded:** 1987 **Current capacity:** 11,000 **Month:** March **Camping:** No **Nearest airport:** Austin **First headliner:** King's X **Recent headliners:** Ice Cube, MGMT, Ferras **Promoter:** SXSW Inc **Website:** www.sxsw.com

YOUROPE

Think back to festival land in the 1970s: the bogs are quite literally bogs, flapping beer tents provide the liquid refreshment, a second-hand plaster is the closest you'd get to first aid and the bill musters the cultural diversity of a BNP march. Fast forward to the twenty-first century and we have luxury toilets (usually adorned with framed hunting scenes), boutique tepees, gourmet cuisine and line-ups boasting musicians from Arkansas to Zanzibar.

The outfit in part responsible for this transmogrification, at least of late, is Yourope, the European Festival Association. The group has been working tirelessly to improve the European festival scene since 1998, collaborating with organisers across the continent to tackle everything from working conditions, health and safety, marketing and sponsorship to the promotion and exchange of musical talent.

Green issues are top of the agenda: Yourope has launched a raft of environmental guidelines, created an online tool delivering customised advice to festival organisers and set up a green award. The prevaricating punter benefits too; working with Virtual Festivals, Yourope has launched a pan-European festival portal – eu.virtualfestivals.com – that aims to showcase more than 3,000 events across 45 countries.

Some 54 festivals have signed up to the association, all boasting top-notch programming, production and audience facilities. Members include Ireland's Oxegen, the UK's Download, Italy's Italia Wave Love Festival, Spain's Benicàssim and Scotland's T In The Park. www.yourope.org/yourope_festivals.aspx

ZZZ...

fter all that jumping around, foot stomping, trudging through mud, cider drinking, rough-housing with strange men in felt mushroom hats and general higher level of physical activity than is wise for most of us, it's time for bed. Unless, of course, you're one of those nutters who decide you'll keep going from the moment you arrive onsite on Thursday night until you're dragged kicking and screaming from your sleeping bag on Tuesday morning just before security start bulldozing the leftover tents.

'Bed' at a festival rarely involves traditional sleeping paraphernalia such as pillows, duvets and sheets. They're as rare as hens' teeth at most campsites, with punters instead opting for a hotchpotch of hastily bought scratchy blankets and damp, mildewed sleeping bags that they forgot to air after that particularly wet T In The Park a few years back. Oops. And after all that, there's the desperate urge to urinate as soon as you slip into your sleeping bag and that annoying little kid in the next-door tent deciding it's time to wake up and test out his lungs. Jesus.

For those with bigger wallets, the festival circuit does now offer so-called 'boutique' camping of a higher order. Wine and dine in a Winnebago, trance out in a teepee or choose between an array of beach huts, Airstreams, Podpads and Myhabs (and that's before the names get really silly). Must be time for bed. Zzzzzzzzz.